W9-DFP-750

Contents

MURDER n. 1. Homicide with malice afore-thought; as legally defined, the unlawful killing of a human being, by a person of sound mind, by an act causing death within a year and a day thereafter, with premeditated malice.

Century Dictionary and Cyclopedia, 1902

Acknowledgments

This venture into the background of the famous Gillette Case represents a total of eighteen years of effort involving two people. Very little of this work fell into the realm of "nine to five," and much of it represents a labor of love that was accomplished in spare time and weekends. This is not the first exploration of the Gillette case; it is not the largest effort of its kind; it is not likely to be the last.

I am indebted to countless others whose help has made this book possible. Outstanding are the Cortland County Historical Society and the Herkimer County Historical Society. Each of these institutions has opened its doors and helped in every possible way. Very little of the following account would exist without them. The story has emerged from the documents of many agencies and a trail of libraries that includes the Library of Congress, the New York City Public Library, the Cortland Free Library and countless university libraries across the Northeast.

Again and again individuals have gone out of their way to assist. Wilda Bowers of South Otselic has provided photographs, clippings and genealogical data. Leonora Brown has shared her many mementos in a most generous manner. I owe much to Dr. Robert C. Williams for glimpses into life on the Brown farm over eighty years ago.

Over the years students and visitors have provided encouragement and direction. I am especially grateful to Phyllis Baldwin, Robert Caplan and Craig Brandon who provided curiosity, intensity and enthusiasm in that order.

My wife, Kae, has endured long hours of listening and reading, has contributed critical opinions when they were most needed, and has suffered many an impromptu detour in reaching remote field sites related to the case. Her patience has been endless. My fellow researcher and writer, Patricia Wawrzaszek has covered miles of field travel dealing with all aspects of the story and hours of writing on chapters 16 and 17.

Finally, one must acknowledge the person who started this more than fifteen years ago—the anonymous colleague whose casual (and incorrect) statement over morning coffee about "that famous drowning" sparked a search that is still going on.

JWB

This project has truly been a labor of love. Countless miles and unimaginable reams of research material have been utilized to make *Adirondack Tragedy* a reality. There remains, though, an insatiable drive for continued research and discovery. Questions only lead to more questions and the adventure will continue. Just as Chester Gillette pursued his dream, so will we pursue the dream of resolving the unanswered queries.

My personal reward has been attained through the friendship of Joe and Kae Brownell. They opened their home and hearts to an inquisitive stranger. The result has been a remarkable sharing of warmth and mutual vitality.

The perseverance to continue with this project is a direct result of the values my parents instilled in me. Responsibility, a sense of obligation and the pursuit of education is their legacy to me. For unquestioning support and an always ready hug, I thank Nancy. A sister and friend is truly a rare combination and Nancy epitomizes both.

Adirondack Tragedy will expand and develop. There is always another piece of the puzzle to fit into its proper place. The authors will continue to prod failing memories and break down the walls of silence that continue to remain. Time and distance, though, may prove to be an advantage. Enjoyment and curiosity were the driving forces behind this work. May they also be the reward we share with our readers.

PAW

Introduction

As June turned into July in 1906 Chester Gillette and Grace Brown were two young people living in Cortland, New York. Few people knew the young man and woman and fewer still knew from where they had come. Even friends would have been reluctant to suggest that their names and reputations would persist for the rest of the then-new century. This is the story of that unusual couple, a story that has gradually turned into legend.

1

A GLORIOUS FOURTH

In July of 1906 Cortland, New York was a city of 15,000. It was small, dusty and somewhat off the main line, high in the valleys of the Appalachian Plateau. But it was a city that was pleased with itself. It was a county seat. It was one of ten towns the state had selected as normal school sites, and the forty year old Cortland Normal was already an institution. The city still received new residents by way of European immigration, it was host to many small and diverse industries, and only recently it had ceased being a village and was operating in the first decade of its brand new city charter.

Mostly, Cortlandites were pleased with the results of the Industrial Revolution which had changed the face of the town in barely half a century. The main street was paved and flanked by four-story business blocks of brick, many with false facades. (The city fathers were still arguing over the priorities of the lesser streets.) Horse cars had given way to the newest form of public transportation—the electric streetcar or trolly.

Streetcar tracks connected Main Street with both railroad stations. The cars themselves had been built right in Cortland and the citizens rather took it for granted that in this age of invention almost anything could be built in factories, if not in Cortland, then certainly somewhere in the United States.

Cortland was not in the main stream; yet, it was *part* of the nation. People accepted the first and were proud of the second. They knew what was happening. A president had been assassinated. Fire and earthquake had destroyed San Francisco. In New York City millionaire playboy Harry Thaw had just been charged with murder. It seemed appropriate—he had shot the famous architect, Stanford White, in front of New York's highest society only two weeks before. Mrs. Thaw, the subject of the clash, was former showgirl Evelyn Nesbit.

The development of the telegraph and the news services made such events a matter of evening reading on the day that they happened. The *Cortland Standard* had, within the past ten years, grown from a weekly to a daily publication. National and local news shared the same pages, but the "big" news was in the national columns. Nothing earthshaking happened in Cortland. About this there was universal agreement.

The city in early July throbbed with the excitement of anticipation, for this was the eve of the most popular secular holiday of the year. The Fourth of July took a back seat to no other day—not even Decoration Day—and the fact that it would fall on a Wednesday in 1906 diminished none of the excitement. The Fourth would be a fabulous holiday. That was a matter of faith.

The day before, Tuesday, was warm and sultry. The tree-lined residential streets of the small city buzzed with the lazy song of the locust. Noisy automobiles were still a rarity, but most people kept horses and every house had a back barn. Boys, out of school for the summer, had bicycles and slingshots. Mostly they had big ideas about the coming holiday. While the previous weekend had registered one of the heaviest downpours in recent history, the Fourth was expected to be perfect.

And so, like every other community in America, Cortland braced for the big event, a holiday that in 1906 seemed to bring together all of the elements of Veterans Day, Labor Day and Halloween. Bunting appeared on Main Street and merchants vied with one another to decorate their store fronts in national colors.

Some feared the worst. Warnings were broadcast (in print) about the dangers of toy guns, real guns and firecrackers. There was certain to be a national death toll from drowning, explosions and accidental shootings. (As it happened there were fifty-one deaths in the nation, but none in Cortland.) For days prior to the Fourth the chief of police ran a notice warning citizens that absolutely no firecrackers were permitted before the evening of the third. The notice ran every year and every year it was disregarded.

Indeed, the holiday began to take shape as workers came home Tuesday afternoon. Plans were made and luggage was packed. The extent of one's activity depended mainly on age and financial status.

Small boys were less interested in speeches than in firecrackers that they had hoarded. For those who could not afford fireworks there was other, if less legal, activity. Forbidden bonfires appeared on the night of the third, fueled by wooden articles that disappeared one by one from homes and businesses. Even the Methodist Church was an unwilling participant—it lost its long wooden ladder.

For adults the limiting factor was money. The well-to-do took all-day rail excursions to popular lake shores in New York and Pennsylvania. These excursion trains left early on the holiday morning and each returned, hopefully with its entire party, after dark.

The young and less fortunate stayed in Cortland County. Churches and lodges sponsored a wide range of events complete with decorating contests, games, oratory and fireworks. In some groups drinking was an implied objective but the WCTU outing promised strict abstinence. Something was planned for everyone. The one question heard most often was "What are you going to do tomorrow?"

Two young people toyed with this very question when they met on Main Street on Tuesday afternoon. One was Chester Gillette, a darkly handsome young man of twenty two who had lived in Cortland just over a year. He worked in the stockroom of his uncle's skirt factory a mile away and he was making a tour of Main Street on the eve of the great holiday.

The other was Harriet Benedict, daughter of a prominent local lawyer. Hattie Benedict was reputed to be the prettiest girl in town and she had caught Chester's eye the winter before. They had met casually several times during the year, usually at Normal School functions. They had been together in foursomes during half-day trips to neighboring resorts, but Chester had never formally called at her home.

She admitted to having no plans for the Fourth and Chester extended a dinner invitation. They might travel to a nearby lake resort for a midday meal. There was one stipulation. She would have to return before the supper hour and Chester promised that they would. The date was made.

There was a feeling of relief in the city as the Fourth finally dawned. Aside from the firecrackers and bonfires, the night before had been a quiet one. On the other hand the early morning showers which dampened the excursion crowds at the rail stations showed promise of tapering off. The deluge of the past Saturday would not be repeated.

13

Indeed, by midmorning the sun broke through and several thousand picnickers left home. Some walked to church yards or the park surrounding the Normal School. Others crowded onto open streetcars. By noon it was clear and temperatures were in the seventies. It was, indeed, a glorious Fourth!

Chester and Hattie started out at midday. By then the heavy traffic on the street cars had slackened a bit, but the company was enjoying one of its best days ever and the cars were still nearly full.

There was some reason for this. The traction company made but a skimpy profit from its normal routes in Cortland and on the two short lines that connected with Homer and McGraw. But there was money to be made from excursion traffic if they could connect with a lake shore.

Fortunately, a popular resort already existed at Little York Lake eight miles north of the city and only five miles north of the streetcar turnaround in Homer. A simple extension of rails was made up the valley in 1905 and the company built a large picnic pavilion on the lake shore. It was rushed to completion in the spring of 1906 and was an instant hit on Memorial Day. Now it was officially open and most of the residents of the city seemed to be planning a holiday picnic at the lake.

Chester and Hattie boarded a car on Main Street. There was little wait, for half-hour service was in operation during daylight hours and would continue for the rest of the summer. Chester's salary was ten dollars a week but transportation was cheap—twenty five cents round trip—and the bulk of his investment could go toward dinner.

The couple rode to the end of the line. Here the pavilion was crowded with excited picnickers drawn by the promise of a band concert. Chester rented a canoe and paddled Harriet across the lake to the Raymond House. This was an older establishment which pre-dated trolly service and now profited from it. The Raymond was a small resort hotel where tourists could stay, rent boats and generally enjoy the lake. It was also a popular eating spot for the "carriage trade" of the community and most of the patrons did, indeed, come in horse drawn rigs. Chester had a taste for the good life and it is here that he brought Harriet, leaving the red canoe at the Raymond dock.

While waiting for a table, Hattie signed the guest register. It wasn't required—they weren't registering at the hotel—but all the local people did it. Moreover, as all the young people knew, the guest list (including diners) was sent on to the *Cortland Standard*

The Raymond House at Little York in 1906. Although it accepted overnight guests it was best known locally for its dining room. Little York Lake lies out of sight behind the house

where it appeared as a social note.

Then, as now, there was a youthful scramble to get one's name in the newspaper and young people played games with the system. Hattie wrote down both their names and after "Chester Gillette" she added "San Francisco." If they hoped to find this titillating addition in the newspaper next day they were to be disappointed. Somewhere between Little York and the pressroom the list was laundered. Chester and Hattie would appear in the paper as perfectly ordinary local residents.[1]

The meals at the Raymond were good but it was the company that was impressive. The couple dined among some of Cortland's best families. To be sure they were not Vanderbilts, Livingstons or Schuylers, but they were the solid upper middle class people of the community. Later it took less than a half hour to return to Cortland. The cars were crowded and the riders were tired but it *was* the end of a perfect holiday, full of youthful, innocent exuberance.

Who could have foreseen that before the end of the month Chester would be jailed on a charge of murder? By the end of the year the names of both would appear in newspapers across the country. Before a generation had passed the events of this month and this year would form the nucleus of one of America's most famous novels.

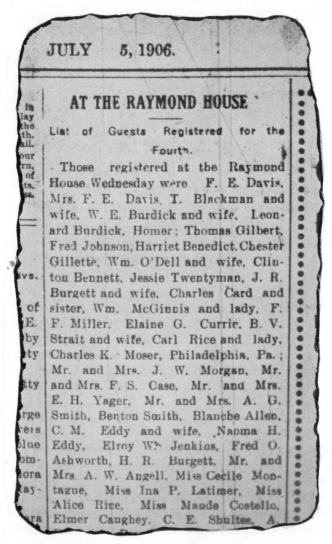

JULY 5, 1906.

AT THE RAYMOND HOUSE

List of Guests Registered for the Fourth.

Those registered at the Raymond House Wednesday were F. E. Davis, Mrs. F. E. Davis, T. Blackman and wife, W. E. Burdick and wife, Leonard Burdick, Homer; Thomas Gilbert, Fred Johnson, Harriet Benedict, Chester Gillette, Wm. O'Dell and wife, Clinton Bennett, Jessie Twentyman, J. R. Burgett and wife, Charles Card and sister, Wm. McGinnis and lady, F. F. Miller, Elaine G. Currie, B. V. Strait and wife, Carl Rice and lady, Charles K. Moser, Philadelphia, Pa.; Mr. and Mrs. J. W. Morgan, Mr. and Mrs. F. S. Case, Mr. and Mrs. E. H. Yager, Mr. and Mrs. A. G. Smith, Benton Smith, Blanche Allen, C. M. Eddy and wife, Naoma H. Eddy, Elroy W. Jenkins, Fred O. Ashworth, H. R. Burgett, Mr. and Mrs. A. W. Angell, Miss Cecile Montague, Miss Ina P. Latimer, Miss Alice Rice, Miss Maude Costello, Elmer Caughey, C. E. Shultes, A.

A recurring social note in the *Cortland Standard* was the list of guests taken from the Raymond House register. Harriet Benedict's entry for herself and Chester appeared in the paper the next day, but the facetious reference to San Francisco was carefully omitted.

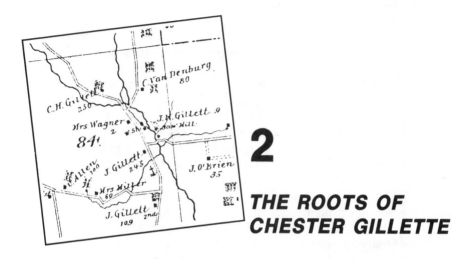

2

THE ROOTS OF
CHESTER GILLETTE

Like a wild New England blizzard whose origins are traced to a small Oregon coastal storm five days earlier, Chester Gillette's tragedy had its beginnings in another time and place. Chester's life was largely influenced by the decision of a grandparent who chose to leave New York and follow the frontier across the continent. If Chester had only recently arrived in New York State in 1905 it was but the completion of a cycle. For more than a century Gillettes had lived in Cortland County and Chester was related to most of them.

The first Gillette came to the county prior to 1800 and the next two generations multiplied and went forth—but usually not far. Most Gillettes were farmers in the town of Scott in an age prior to commercial farming in New York State.* This meant living at a near-subsistence level, but this was true of farmers throughout upstate New York. Only a few descendants moved to the village of Cortland ten miles away.

There were alternatives and some Gillettes chose them. A few entered business either as tradesmen or as sawmillers. But they stayed in the villages and hamlets close by the town of Scott. Once in a while a Gillette left the state to seek a new life in the Middle West, thereby setting a precedent for future generations. As the Civil War

---

*New York State follows the New England practice of calling the smallest rural political unit a town. Elsewhere in the United States it would be a township.

loomed in mid century there was a cluster of farms on the hilly soils of Scott, each bearing the family name.[1]

The original New England Gillette was reputed to have been a French Huguenot, but the descendants who came to Cortland County were ordinary Protestant farmers, indistinguishable from their neighbors of English or Scottish descent. For most of the nineteenth century the family spelled the name *Gillett* without the final "e." The spelling change may have been an accident. It may also have been an attempt to Anglicize a surname which, to rural New Yorkers of the day, looked uncomfortably alien.

The taproot of Chester's own family tree was his grandfather, Albertus Gillette. Born in 1822, he grew up with his many cousins among the farms and sawmills of East Scott. In the 1840s Albertus married Harriet Osborne, a Cortland County girl, and in a span of 13 years the young couple produced a family of five: Rembrandt, Frank S., Noah Horace, Carrie Nina, and the youngest, Ellsworth P.[2]

The family appeared to be complete in 1861 and the Civil War affected neither the father who was too old for service, nor the sons who were too young. It was a tightly knit home at the end of the war, with children ranging from five to seventeen—a typical mid-nineteenth century upstate family, seemingly destined to spend a lifetime on a rural New York farm.

But something happened. Albertus took his entire family on a twenty year odyssey that ended in the Pacific Northwest. The reasons for his abrupt removal to the West are a matter of speculation. The lure of the frontier was a long standing tradition and the attractions of the West were already being amplified in the press. Land, too, may have been a factor. The prolific Gillettes were beginning to put something of a strain on the farms that their ancestors had carved out of Cortland County forests. The homestead act of 1862 (or at least the public interpretation of it) promised land, and even more land, west of the Mississippi.

There is even a suggestion that health may have prompted the Albertus Gillette family to trek westward. In humid upstate New York the annual rainfall approaches forty inches. For nearly thirty years prior to his death Albertus took his family to places of high elevation and dry climate. Rarely did the precipitation of these sites exceed fourteen inches. For whose benefit, if any, such moves were made is unclear.

Getting west was easier said than done—even in that heyday of railroad construction. East of the Mississippi the rail network was dense and service was frequent. Diamond stack woodburners were rapidly giving way to fast coal-fired engines. But in the West most lines ended between the Mississippi and the Missouri. Beyond Omaha in 1870, only the newly completed Union Pacific stretched across the plains and mountains to Utah, but the Gillettes were destined for Montana.

The public believed in the railroads and it wanted badly to believe in westward expansion. The gaudy railroad timetables were graced with maps that showed new lines extending west like the tentacles of an octopus. But beyond the Mississippi and Red rivers these map symbols were more apt to represent expectation than reality. *Red River runs N to S in Louisiana*

Albertus Gillette's pilgrimage more or less paralleled the westward march of these frontier railroads, and particularly that of the Northern Pacific. That line was chartered just before the end of the Civil War when Albertus, himself, was beginning to "Think West." By 1870 the Northern Pacific began laying track westward from Minneapolis and by 1871 it had reached the Red River of the North. The panic of 1873 stopped all construction on the line just after it had come to Bismark, Dakota Territory, and rails were not laid again until 1878. Seattle was still a thousand miles away.

The road then progressed rapidly up the Yellowstone Valley toward western Montana, but by then the Gillette family was already there, in the mining district outside Helena. Albertus had taken the hard route to the Montana Territory—rail, stagecoach and foot. He now had a proper western address—Wickes, Montana—just twenty miles south of the bustling city of Helena.

Wickes lay nestled in the foothills and low mountains that rose to the continental divide only a few miles away. Elevations were high and rainfall was low, but the slopes of the mountains supported stands of pine. The mountain rock offered a variety of mineral ores.

Wickes was a burst-at-the-seams mining town. Money flowed freely and activity was divided among mining, lumbering, business and even some ranching. Many of the mines required timber for shoring. Logging was natural to those who had come from Cortland County and most of the Gillette men found surface jobs that dealt with timber. At its peak the little mining town had a population that exceeded 2,000.

Despite the rough and ready frontier life, the Gillettes maintained eastern values toward education. All of the children attended classes in whatever schools were available. The older boys went directly to work in the local community but as the two youngest children approached adulthood the family made a decision. Carrie Nina and Ellsworth were sent east for education beyond the grammar school level.

The modern public high school had not yet emerged in 1880 and the East teemed with preparatory schools and academies, almost all of which were private. Carrie and Ellsworth both attended the preparatory division of Oberlin College.[3] Carrie appears to have demonstrated a musical talent, for after one year in preparatory division she spent a second in Oberlin Conservatory. By 1883 both young people had returned to the family in Montana.

While the two youngest were away at school, the second son, Frank, met a local school teacher in Wickes. Little is known about Louise Rice except that she was born in Massachusetts and that she was a person of great motivation and strong character. Frontier people usually were. Almost no one in the territory at that time had been born there—they had elected to live where they were, and something had drawn Louise Rice to western Montana.

Old timers would later tell how Louise was once rescued from a runaway mule by Frank Gillette. While this is probably not how they met, they did spend the rest of Frank's life together, for they were married in 1882. Carrie and Rembrandt were witnesses.[4]

In 1883 they had their first child, a boy whom they named Chester Ellsworth. Chester may have been a common name in the Rice family but Ellsworth came directly from the baby's youngest Gillette uncle.

As a young man, Chester often complained that he was the victim of the system, of ineptitude and of plain bad luck. There may have been some justice to his claim, for the records of vital statistics kept in Jefferson county, Montana would seem to have conspired against him from the start.

While Chester was born in August of 1883, the records purport that his parents were married three months later in October! But it was a mistake—a very human mistake. Records were rarely kept at that time and the minister who performed the ceremony for Frank and Louise Gillette in October of 1882 did not appear at the county recorder's office until the spring of 1883 when he recorded a recent ceremony and added the five-month-old Gillette wedding as well. Unfortunately the writer did what many of us do—he wrote down the current year (1883) rather than the actual one. Chester was, in fact, born a very proper nine and one half months after his parents were married.[5]

20

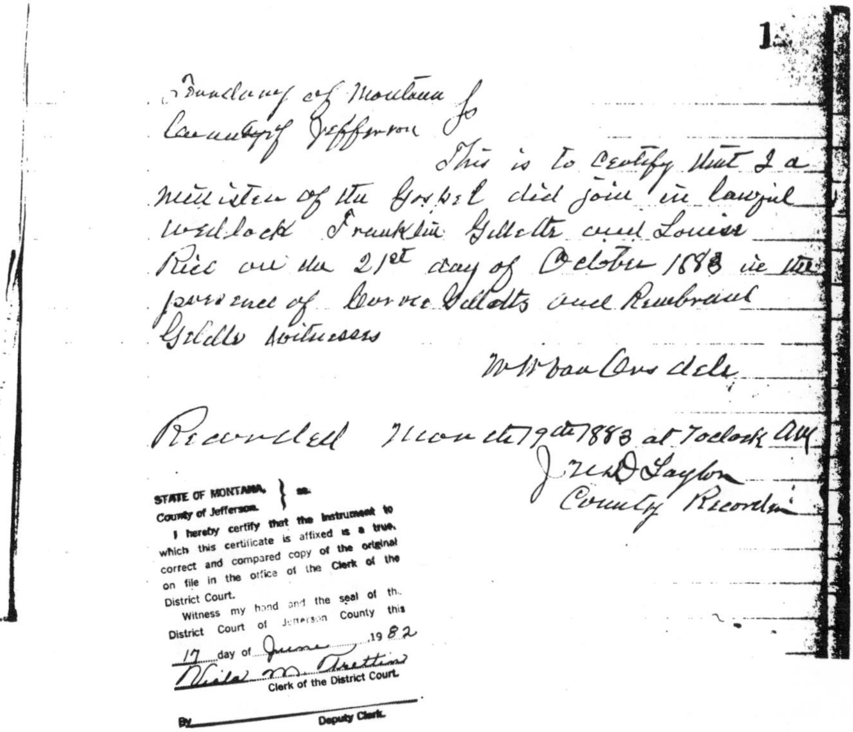

1

Territory of Montana }
County of Jefferson } ss

This is to Certify that I a minister of the Gospel did join in lawful wedlock Franklin Gillette and Louise Rice on the 21st day of October 1883 in the presence of Horace Gillette and Rembrant Gillette witnesses

W W Van Orsdele

Recorded March 9th 1883 at 7 oclock AM

J W D Taylor
County Recorder

STATE OF MONTANA, } ss.
County of Jefferson.

I hereby certify that the instrument to which this certificate is affixed is a true, correct and compared copy of the original on file in the office of the Clerk of the District Court.

Witness my hand and the seal of the District Court of Jefferson County this 17 day of June 1982

Clerk of the District Court.

By ________ Deputy Clerk.

Marriage record from the District Court of Jefferson County, Boulder, Montana, as entered by County Recorder J. W. D. Taylor. Note the date 1882 was recorded as 1883 by mistake and that the minister is apparently W. W. Van Orsdele.

3

AN HORATIO ALGER IN CORTLAND

The tight little family of Albertus Gillette knew one defector who left the West. It was the third son, Noah Horace. Male children have for years been burdened with the names of grandfathers and Noah Horace was linked to both sides of the family. His mother's father was Noah Humphrey Osborne and his father's father was Horatio N. Gillette. (See endpiece)

There is little that small boys can do about names they do not like and this one appeared not to like the name Noah. But by the time he was an adult he carefully listed himself as N. Horace Gillette and in later years friends knew him simply as "Horace" and even as "N. H."

Horace left the westward-bound family in 1876 and returned to the East. He did not merely return to New York State—he disappeared into the maw of New York City and stayed there for nearly twenty years. This young man who had traveled to the West as a child and gained only the basic education of available schools was destined to become a success story in the Gillette family. Through hard work he emerged as a polished, wealthy gentlemen just like the fictional characters of Horatio Alger.

But the heros of Horatio Alger needed more than hard work. Inevitably the storybook character was befriended by a well-placed member of society. This mentor guided the young waif and sometimes gave financial assistance as well. Horace Gillette, too, was gifted with an angel and in his case by a relative.

Horace's mother had been an Osborne and her sister (Horaces's

23

aunt) had married Dr. Lucien Warner back in Cortland County, New York. This enterprising young physician and his brother were making a comfortable living lecturing on health and hygiene.

Dr. Warner had gone to Oberlin College and was an extremely proud alumnus. It was probably through correspondence between the Osborne sisters that the two younger Gillettes had been sent to Oberlin Preparatory School. By that time Dr. Warner had established a profitable business and, no doubt, aided his niece and nephew with the expenses of an education in Ohio. He was later to become an active member of the Oberlin board, and donated a substantial building to the college.

In 1874 this was still in the future. The two Warner brothers had just developed a "health corset" as an adjunct to their winter health lectures. A health corset was long overdue since the styles of the day ran to narrow waists that threatened to pinch the wearer in two. While lecturing made the Warner brothers a good living, the new corset would be an item for sale in halls and auditoriums during the winter speaking tours. They commenced the manufacture of these garments in the little village of McGrawville (now McGraw) only a few miles from the farm that Albertus Gillette had left shortly before.[1]

In 1874 the newly married Lucien Warner left his brother in McGraw and moved to New York City with his bride, hoping to establish a medical practice. Medicine in lower Manhattan was a dismal failure, but the corset turned out to be a product in demand.

Lucien found that his central position in New York City was a great asset. He could purchase raw materials and see to the completion of partly finished garments started in McGraw. Moreover, the corset supply they had intended to sell personally on winter speaking tours rapidly disappeared into the hands of salesmen who left New York City to cover the northeastern territories. Lucien abandoned medicine altogether and became a businessman.

The Warners found themselves with a small but booming industry half of which was in upstate New York and half in a New York City apartment. Even as they contemplated moving the business into a Broadway loft, the newlyweds sought assistance. In 1876 they hired Mrs. Warner's nephew, Horace, to take over much of the clerical, sales and promotional part of the business in the new Broadway head office.[2] The young man with western dust on his boots plunged into big business and city living. He worked in the

Broadway office which became the firm's business headquarters. In a short time the production facilities were removed from McGrawville and relocated in a spacious new plant in Bridgeport, Connecticut.[3]

From the very first Horace was a vital part of Warner Brothers. At the start he knew nothing about women's garments, but he had a natural grasp of figures and he worked closely with the sales organizations that sold the Warner product. During his stay in New York City he was referred to as a salesman, clerk, corresponding secretary, bookkeeper, merchant and commercial traveler. His obituary many years later may have offered the greatest clue to his business character when it called him "One of the best credit men in the business."[4] He learned the garment trade while Warner Brothers enjoyed his skill—it was quite an even match.

During his career in the big city Horace Gillette slowly worked his way up the middle class ladder. In the early, unmarried, years he was content to live near the company offices. He had come to town a western bachelor, but he was to leave as a suburban family man with beard and mustache.

In 1882 he married Caroline Rice of Scranton, Pennsylvania.[5] Carrie Rice was the daughter of a Methodist minister who was quite happy to marry the young couple himself, and in his own home. The marriage threatened to confuse future biographers, for this was the second Carrie in Horace's life. His sister, Carrie Nina, was still in Montana. Moreover, both Horace and his brother Frank married girls named Rice. Were Rice not a common name the coincidence might invite suspicion, but the two girls appear to have been unrelated.

Marriage meant a different way of life and Horace took his new bride to live in New Jersey. It was just becoming fashionable to live in the suburbs—indeed the railroads were then creating the suburbs—and their North Plainfield house was only a short walk from the station.[6] On Manhattan the ferry slip was another short walk from the office.* It was an hour's travel each way, but commuters were willing to endure it. In the 1880s the American middle class was already creating the pattern for a future society of commuters.

In 1887 Horace moved again, this time to Brooklyn. The newly-

---

*Railroads approaching New York City from New Jersey stopped at the Hudson River. All passengers continued by ferryboat.

opened Brooklyn Bridge was changing the patterns of New York commuters and their suburbs. The graceful city of Brooklyn had long been a desirable place for the middle class, but like New Jersey the link to New York was by slow ferryboat. Now the bridge offered a rapid connection to lower Manhattan and Horace moved with the tide. He lived in two different houses with Brooklyn addresses.[7,8]

His family was growing. A son, Harold, had been born in New Jersey and now a daughter, Dorothy, arrived in Brooklyn.[9] In the last of the Brooklyn years his wife's parents came to live with them. At least two of the Rice sons now lived in New York too, but Carrie's parents moved in with the Gillettes.

It looked as if Horace would become a permanent Brooklyn resident. His position in New York was secure. He and Carrie selected the "proper" church and became staunch Congregationalists (Although Carrie's father, who was living with them, was a retired Methodist minister). Along with the Rices, the Gillettes selected a family plot in the new Cyprus Hills cemetery. Horace was putting down roots.

But in 1895 he abruptly left Warner Brothers to work for a corset company in McGrawville, N.Y. He departed with his wife, children and Carrie's parents to live in the small village where Lucien Warner and his brother had started making corsets twenty years before. He was now back in Cortland County, which he had left as a child. His part of the family had now come full circle.

Horace stayed in the little village just one year. He then moved to nearby Cortland and established a company of his own. By now he knew the garment business well. He sensed that the nipped-waist era of corsets was coming to an end and instead, designed a line of women's skirts. The first factory was in a small building but he hired well, set up a good purchasing system and relied heavily on the sales networks which he had come to know so well in New York City. It worked. In just a year the little business outgrew its space and moved to a second floor location on Clinton Street.

By 1899 a second move was necessary and this time the firm, now known as the Gillette Skirt Company, occupied an entire wooden factory building on the northern edge of the city. Again the gods of success beamed on Horace Gillette and his small company quickly became one of the better industries in Cortland.[10]

In January of 1904 the factory building caught fire and burned in a snowstorm. Typically, the fire companies arrived late and worked without adequate equipment. All that was left of the Gillette Skirt Company were a few large wooden beams from the barn-like structure, and a detached bicycle shelter.[11]

The original wooden factory building which burned in 1904

Large, square timbers in the attic of the former Gillette Skirt Factory show signs of severe charring. They were probably taken from the wreckage of the previous building.

For two months the city wondered if Gillette would rebuild. He, too, seemed to have doubts, for other communities were attempting to solicit his business. But by summer he had committed himself to Cortland and commenced a new and modern factory building. Perhaps because of the fire he attempted to make the building "fireproof" using the newest methods and materials.

The building was fashioned from concrete blocks, a new concept in 1904. The blocks were cast right on the construction site and were shaped to resemble stone. Like most early attempts it failed. They still looked like concrete blocks. The cornerstone of the building proudly proclaimed the name of the firm and cited the historic use of the new concrete blocks.[12]

The inner floors and stanchions, however, were of wood and their painted surfaces would have been a severe test to Gillette's hope of a fireproof building, but fortunately they were never tested.

The former Gillette Skirt Factory from the southeast. Horace Gillette's office was located on the main floor in the near corner. Next to his office is a missing window where the walk-in vault was situated. Chester worked in the sunken first floor which at this end of the building served as the stockroom. Grace worked in the cutting room at the left, or west end of the floor. Insert shows the cornerstone of the building, the first built of concrete blocks in Cortland dated 1904.

The main office force at the Gillette Skirt Factory. Mr. Gillette appears in the service window in the rear.

N. H. Gillette in his private office in the southeast corner of the first floor of the new factory building.

New materials were used everywhere in an effort to be up-to-date. There was one small exception. The vertical beams supporting the attic roof were made from timbers that remained after the fire and their charred sides stood out in contrast to the new wood and concrete surfaces.

In New York City success in the garment trade depended on cheap immigrant labor, a fact that Horace had learned years before. In Cortland, immigrant labor was more apt to be found among the male employees of heavy industries and in construction. Gillette turned to native born factory girls recruited from the local area. They were cutters, sewing machine operators and stockroom workers. They worked for extremely modest wages, meeting the need for extra cash in the family.

Yet Gillette was remarkably innovative for his day. More often than not department heads in the factory were women. Some were married, others were not. Many of today's businesses have poorer records of women in management.

In its best years the factory employed nearly two hundred people on the premises and used several hundred canvassers in the field.[13] These salespeople, however, probably served more than one master and merely took on the Gillette skirt as part of their "line."

N. H. Gillette's home at 20 West Court Street in Cortland served for many years as a sorority house before it was torn down in 1956.

There was an annual picnic for employees at which every worker was a guest. But the department heads were treated separately to more formal functions in the Gillette home.

The family life of the Gillettes was generally private. While they entertained close friends and key factory personnel, it was not a family which entertained often or lavishly. Indeed few of the well-to-do people of upstate Cortland were caught up in a giddy round of night life and spending. The waning Victorian era was still to be felt here.

On coming to Cortland, Horace moved to a large house on West Court Street—a wooden house with graceful arches and a round portico. It was the only one like it in Cortland. It was a desirable location across from the Henry Randall house. (Locals would have said: 'The Henry Randall House!') Large though it was, it did not rank with the huge Wickwire houses only two streets away, for Horace was more practical than pretentious. His home was within a block of the city center and a minute's walk from the trolley line that went past the factory, located a mile to the north.

His involvement in community affairs might seem limited by twentieth century standards but was typical for men of his day. He was a Mason (a carryover from Brooklyn) and an automobile enthusiast. He and friends often went to New York City by train to take in the annual auto show.

Horace considered church membership an important part of his community association and promptly joined the "right" church once more, only this time it was the Presbyterian Church to which most of the influential members of the community belonged.

Like many self made men he read avidly and did partake of one activity out of sheer enjoyment. He was a founder and member of the Science Club. This was a study group composed of townsmen with a taste for the wonders of modern science and engineering. As might be expected, several of its members were from the Normal School and faculty members were often invited to present topics that ranged from Darwin to the harnessing of the Niagara River.

In just five years Horace had become one of the best known men of town—a man to admire and emulate. His branch of the family had restored the final "e" to its name, and N. H. came from New York City that way. In short order most of the city's Gilletts added the final "e" to *their* names.

His family was modestly large. By 1900 when the factory first moved into large quarters he had a household of eight including a live-in servant.[14] Mrs. Gillette directed the management of the house and even indulged in an outside activity. She was a member of the Daughters of the American Revolution and sometimes represented the local chapter at conventions. Her mother and father had come to Cortland with the family but both were aging and neither would live three years into the new century.

The last person in the family was a nephew from Montana. Horace had assumed, or at least tolerated, the role of rich relative to many of the Gillette clan. His factory was staffed by many of his own cousins, from Ella Hoag, a superintendent, to Frank B. Gillette, Ella's brother, who was an operating engineer. Both were first cousins.

Perhaps, then, it was in keeping with tradition that Horace took in his nephew. (According to some reports he adopted the boy.) Leslie Gillette's parents are unknown except that he was born in Montana of a New York father and a Virginia mother. He was born in 1884, a year after Chester was born (also in Montana) to Frank and Louise Gillette, and a year before Horace's own son Harold, was born in New Jersey.[15]

Either Rembrandt, the oldest brother, or Ellsworth, the youngest, might have been the parent although it is not certain that either one married. Leslie will remain something of a mystery but he did set a precedent. Horace had befriended a nephew from the western branch of the family. He would do it again.

4

A GIRL
CALLED BILLY

As grandchildren of Albertus Gillette were born from Montana to Brooklyn, another family was emerging in rural New York State—a family which was to play an important role in the events to come. Frank and Minerva Brown raised their children in the Town of Otselic in Chenango County, New York, only thirty five miles east of Cortland.

It was a small farmhouse, located on a high hill overlooking the Otselic Valley. The house was three miles from the post office in the village of South Otselic in an age when "going for the mail" was one of the highlights of the day. Most neighboring farms were connected to each other and to the village by a network of gravel roads. The locals called them *dirt* roads and they were in a position to know. The highways became great muddy mires during every spring thaw.

The Brown children were all born in the little farmhouse, arriving at intervals from 1876 to 1895.[1] In the end there were nine living children from Carl, the oldest to Ruby the youngest. It was a house full of girls, for Carl had only one brother, but it was the middle child who was destined to become a household name in America. She was Grace, but from an early age her family called her Billy.

As a little girl Billy's earliest memories were of her immediate environment—the farm. It was a life that revolved around the house, the barn, the orchard, the pasture and the hay fields. The two boys were expected to help with plowing and work in the barn. But many

33

Looking west from the Brown farmhouse, the soil was stony
but the view was magnificient.

of the chores were shared by all of the children. There were trips to
the village, work in the garden, work in the orchard and at haying
time the entire family worked in the fields. Grace was never lazy—
no one on a farm could afford to be.

The Browns looked to South Otselic for basic services. But
South Otselic, itself, was an isolated community, for no rail service
extended up the Otselic Valley. To reach the outside world it was
first necessary to walk or drive a team to DeRuyter or to Cincinnatus
where branch lines of the railroad system offered connections to
nearby cities.

Yet by 1900 physical isolation no longer brought with it every
cultural deprivation of the past. Postage was cheap and mail service
was rapid. Parcel Post had been introduced recently and it was now
possible to purchase goods from the great mail order houses of
Albany and Chicago. Public education was beginning to pay its first
large dividend.

Young women in the country avidly studied the magazines that
brought news about current styles and their sewing machines
produced quick copies. The day was fast approaching when the
visible distinctions between city "slickers" and country "hicks"
would disappear altogether. South Otselic may have been isolated
but it was not backward.

The Brown Family Home in South Otselic
As seen on an old postcard

The tempo of the Brown house was that of bustling, busy people, but it was a happy house. Like all farm children they knew that things come in seasonal waves. There were wild berries to be picked in summer, orchard fruit to gather in the fall, snow to shovel in the winter, and "sugaring" in the spring. There was always some kind neighbor who would greet children who appeared in the steaming "sugar house" looking for a taste of sweet maple syrup, hot from the evaporator.

As the children grew older there were parties. Frank and Minerva Brown may seem at first sight to have been stiff and forbidding parents but this was far from true. They were tolerant of their children's friends and often the house would bulge with a Saturday evening party of girls who had known each other at school.

Crowding was inevitable. Eleven people place a strain on any house and the Brown house was rather small when compared to most upstate farmhouses. No one had the luxury of a private room, though in summer some of the older children may have slept outdoors or in the back shed.

By the turn of the century Billy was fourteen and school was a large part of her life. She was an excellent reader and wrote standard school English in a distinctive longhand. School was a half mile away and it was an age when the students walked—both ways. The little

35

The teacher, Maude Kenyon, is pictured in the upper left with the older students of the Tallett Hill School in 1903. Grace Brown stands next to her and on the right is Fern Tallett. Mary Brown stands in front of Miss Kenyon and Frances is in the lower left.

rural school had been built on the edge of Tallett Hill and was known simply as the Tallett Hill School.

By fifteen she was well known in school but at home she struggled for identity like any modern teenager. Her middle name was Mae but in her new diary that year she wrote *G. Mae Browne* complete with a final "e." She was sometimes Grace, sometimes Billy, and in a joke that involved the national folk hero of the day, she often referred to herself as Billy, "The Kid."

Privacy was nearly impossible in the little house, yet she had special friends in whom she could confide. Her next younger sister, Mary, was unusually close, and her much older sister, Ada, was something of a model, although married and living away. Each in her own way offered Grace an opportunity to share secrets.

Students did not stay in school for long in that age and by now Grace was one of the older students. Fern Tallett was a close chum. Fern lived near the school and as in most rural schools of the day the two older girls frequently helped the teacher with the younger children. Perhaps the friendship with Fern became a bit too close at times for the teacher often found it necessary to separate them!

Grace's teacher was Maude Kenyon, a young woman barely

seven years older than Grace. Grace liked Maude but grumbled about her as do all students who watch their teachers through a magnifying glass. Billy's diary was illuminating:

Mar 28
Miss Kenyon has been just awful cross of late. She thinks she is so smart I can't bear her. Papa went to B. M. [Beaver Meadow] and carried my letter. Miss K— got a letter from Dr. Guess that's what makes her so cross. I can stand it though.[2]

Maude Kenyon's "Dr." was young J. Mott Crumb who was preparing for a career in medicine. He was very close to being the teacher's fiance at this time but was limited to writing her letters. Billy and Fern kept constant track of the romance by monitoring Miss Kenyon's every mood.

Being a teenager in the hills of Chenango County was little different from adolescence anywhere else, even in that age. Girls aspired to adult trends in clothing and hairstyle. At the moment the high-piled hair of the Gibson Girl was all the rage. Fern adopted it first but Grace had to wait. Growing up was hardly a painless procedure but even illness could be an occasion:

March 20
Talk about *dramatic scenes.* We had one. I was very ill all night. *Fainted* for the first time in my life.[3]

Grace had good reason to faint—she had been sick for over a day. But it was an age when victorian heroines swooned with hand on forehead in moments of crisis. Grace treated it as an event, perhaps even a rite of passage.

As comfortable as Billy was in the heart of her family, she was beginning to feel fenced in. She could take refuge in her school friendships, but at home she felt restricted. Her greatest pleasure was an extended visit to her older sister Ada. Ada had married Clarence Hawley and lived in Cincinnatus several miles to the south. In Ada's house there were no competing brothers and sisters and Ada, about to have her first child, treated Grace quite as an equal. Moreover, Billy liked Clarence whom she often called "C E" and he, in turn, treated Grace with unusual kindness. When it was time to return home to South Otselic, Grace had mixed feelings:

Mar 7
...the time is almost here when I have got to go home. I don't dread it so much. "Have you your coat on?"[4]

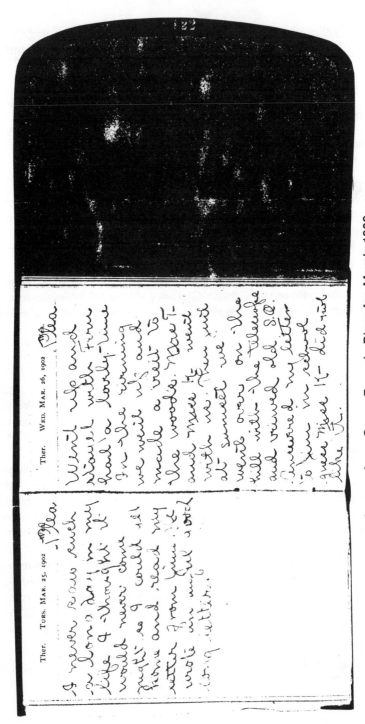

A page from Grace Brown's Diary for March 1902.
Many teenagers kept a diary such as this one of Grace Brown

38

Life in Ada's home seemed just a little less restrictive and Billy may have been tempted to leave home where parents worried about such childish things as wearing overcoats outdoors! But when she went to Norwich next winter to work in a strange home she missed her own family badly:

Dec 14

Have been lonesome all day. Wish I was back on the hill. Am blue. I don't believe I am going to have any Xmas. I am so far from home.[5]

During her last year in the Tallett Hill School Grace and Fern were prone to rate Miss Kenyon much more highly. It was to be Miss Kenyon's last year too, for she left teaching to marry. Her husband was young Dr. Crumb who returned to be the village doctor in South Otselic, a role he would play for many years to come.

Grace had to decide what she was to do with her life for she could not stay on the farm forever. In moments of near privacy she curled up by an upstairs window where she could be by herself on a rainy day. Whatever faults the farm may have had, the view of the lush green valley was magnificent.

And the farm *was* experiencing problems. Since the Civil War a slow and subtle change had come over the rural farmlands of New York State. Until that war eastern farming was largely a subsistence activity. It was not that New York farmers were lacking in skill or desire. They yearned for the cash cropping that had made southern cotton farmers a smart, if ill-fated success. It was just that there was no competitive crop which would grow in the northeast, would sell at market and keep from spoiling until it got there.

Some ten years after the end of the war a wave of rural cheese factory construction began in the state. Cheese, unlike fluid milk, would last during shipment and local farmers could haul their milk short distances to the factories without fear of spoilage. In the seventies and eighties a kind of heyday was enjoyed in rural New York.

In 1875 New York farms nearly reached the wartime peak of 242,000. Then, slowly, the number of farms and farmers declined.[6] Without realizing it, Frank Brown was caught up in this drama of agricultural economics and became one of the statistics.*

---

*By 1950 the number of farms in the state had dropped to half and the trend has accelerated since. In 1970 only 52,000 farms remained in the state.

What had happened? How did the success spawned by the cheese factory end in such failure only a few years later? The answer is that agriculture as an institution did not fail. Instead, it embraced the machines and fuels of the industrial revolution and proceeded to increase production with a vengeance.

The invention of the refrigerated rail car made it possible to ship fluid milk to the giant market of New York City. The daily milk train became part of the rural scene and the language. Today, a fraction of the 1875 farms produces many times the agricultural output for New York State, and does it on even less land than before.

But modern, mechanized farming is not competitive for all operators or on all farmlands. The grim truth is that each year small farms and farms on lesser soils fail. The collapse does not come suddenly. There are years of marginal operation, often supplemented by outside jobs for the owner or his family. Finally the end comes and another farm family enters the general job market, often carrying with it the unwarranted guilt that comes with being the generation which broke one or two centuries of farming tradition.

This pattern which is so common today was already beginning at the turn of the century and Frank Brown was an unwitting victim of such farm abandonment. Like most farmers so victimized he never *intended* to fail. He was a hard-working and skilled farmer. At 215 acres his farm was larger than most and it had done well during the cheese factory era. But by 1900 a mortgage had been foreclosed and Brown leased what had once been his own place.[7] His upland farm was noncompetitive due to distance from the highway, thin soils and rolling surface.

Lack of rail service in the Otselic Valley was an even greater factor, for it would be a half century before the large, but maneuverable, stainless steel tractor trailer would replace the milk train and reach South Otselic. Bit by bit it became harder for Frank Brown to keep pace with his colleagues who were fortunate enough to have flat land in the valley bottoms. As his children grew up, Brown's farm was slowly going down.

For Billy and the other girls in the family the decline may have been imperceptive. Times seemed hard, yet it was axiomatic that the farm lot in rural New York had *always* been hard. For girls the normal expectation was marriage. A married daughter left the house but seldom moved far away. She often remained in the same county.

Ada, of course, had already left. She and Clarence had left Cincinnatus and moved to the city of Cortland where Clarence had found employment.[8] They rented a small house on Fifth Avenue and asked Grace to move in with them and their new son, Robert. Grace was still unmarried, although as a teenager she had once had a "beau" of sorts. When Ada's invitation came Billy quickly accepted.

Nineteen year old Grace quickly found work in the newly completed Gillette Skirt Company where she was soon seen as a pleasant, hard working employee. The pay was but a few dollars a week, but it was more money than she had ever seen back on the farm.

Then in 1905 Ada and her husband suddenly left Cortland, and moved to an eastern part of the county. Grace faced a decision. She had to choose whether to move with Ada, return to the farm, or arrange to live alone in Cortland. She stayed. She moved from Fifth Avenue to the former Wheeler farmhouse on the edge of the city where Mrs. Wheeler took her in as a boarder. Nothing could have been more proper and the walk to work was short—the factory could be seen from the front door.

In a sense Billy was isolated again. Ada had moved away and her family was miles to the east. Although she went home for visits once or twice a year, the journey was long and awkward. As she settled into her new routine she depended more and more on the mails and on her new friends from among the girls at the factory. In April of 1906 she reached her twentieth birthday, but by then her life had taken a new and very different turn.

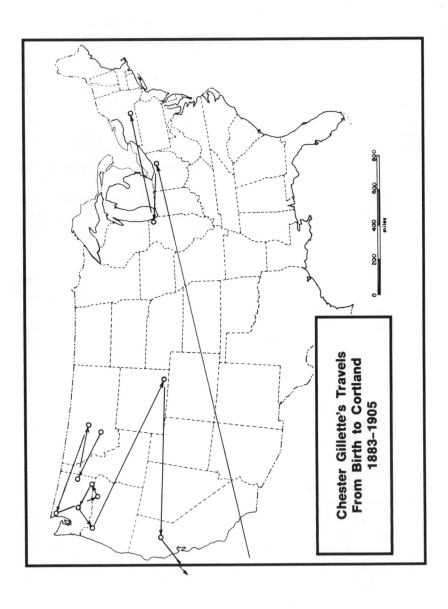

Chester Gillette's Travels
From Birth to Cortland
1883–1905

5

THE BOY FROM THE WEST

Chester was a nomad, although he came by it honestly enough. His grandparents had left the quiet stability of the eastern farm for the bustle of the western frontier. But that was a common, and even acceptable, action in the nineteenth century. At times it seemed as if the whole country was moving west—bag, baggage, and children.

Still, Chester was different. After his birth in 1883 the family stayed in Montana for three more years. Unless the mysterious cousin Leslie was also being reared in Wickes, Chester's earliest memories were those of an only child among grandparents, aunts and uncles. But in 1886 the Gillette family made its last great move—this time to Spokane. Here in the Washington Territory the grandparents stopped, as did the aunts and uncles. And so for the time being did Chester's parents, for they stayed in Spokane until Chester was nearly twelve.

The years in Spokane seemed to have been as American as apple pie. The family lived on streets with numbered houses and Chester went to public schools. Frank Gillette, his father, worked as the operator of a bathhouse and served with a fire company. Two sisters, Hazel and Lucille, were born and finally in 1893 a brother, Paul, completed their family. The family had reached the heights (or perhaps the depths) of stability.[1]

But if Chester's grandparents, aunts and uncles settled down to the traditional life of Spokane, his parents did not. Quite suddenly, in 1894, they responded to the call of the Salvation Army. Whether one was called and the other merely accompanied is not clear, but on January 1, 1895 they both joined the Army together.[2]

In those days the Salvation Army divided the United States into operational areas called provinces. Names and boundaries changed frequently as the Army expanded and as the region became more populated. In 1895 the thinly populated West constituted a single large province. Each province was, itself, divided into divisions and the states and territories of Montana, Idaho, Oregon and Washington made up the Northern Pacific Division.

It was here that the Gillettes entered into Salvation Army life, complete with visored cap and poke bonnet. They were to spend the next months in Great Falls, Montana learning the ropes of missionary Christianity.[3]

The West had always been considered a fertile field for mission work. In the nineteenth century Catholic and Protestant outposts strove for the conversion of the native Americans who were being displaced by "civilization."

They would have done well to place their attention elsewhere. The frontier brought with it miners, cattlemen, fishermen and loggers along with the occasional gold rush participant. Each group brought its share of the sins of civilization. By the 1890s the Salvation Army had targeted these groups along with the problems of the emerging cities. Their battles were against poverty, alcohol and sin.

When the Gillettes were ready for their first assignment they and their four children were sent back to Washington State. The Northern Pacific Division presented a colorful array of place names, for the Army had posts in Missoula, Walla Walla, Olympia, Snohomish and Puyallup. The new assignment was in Whatcom, Washington. Thirteen year old Chester was about to embark on a decade of long journeys, short stays and strange lodgings.

Whatcom lay nestled on Pacific Ocean waters in the damp, forested corner of northwestern Washington between Seattle and Vancouver, Canada.* It was a sharp contrast to the dry lands of Montana and Spokane to which the Gillettes had become so accustomed. But there was much for the Salvation Army to sink its teeth into. The town boasted a colorful role as a wild shipping point during the Yukon gold rush and had inherited the economic lethargy that followed the inevitable bust.

---

*In a scant five years the little city of Whatcom was to merge with its neighbors and change its name to Bellingham.

By the turn of the century Whatcom was full of sawmills and the lumbermen who came and went with them. It was also a budding site for salmon canneries, for the waters of the Pacific Northwest were showing great promise as commercial fishing grounds if only a safe and profitable method of canning the product would appear. Between the poverty of the cannery workers and the rough qualities of the sawmillers, the Gillettes had plenty to do.[4]

In early 1897 Frank and Louise were both promoted to the rank of captain. But the traditions of the Northern Pacific Division called for personnel to be transferred in November and in June and there was little time to enjoy the new rank in Whatcom. In less than six months young Chester found his parents ready to move again.[5]

The next stop was Pendleton, Oregon.[6] The dry plateau of eastern Oregon (less than 14 inches of rain annually) resembled the Spokane environment in which Chester had grown up and stood in sharp contrast to the damp forests near the coast. But like Whatcom, the town was small and the cattlemen of Pendleton had the same rough problems as loggers and sawmillers. While the great cattle barons still existed, the Salvation Army was more interested in the lives of the ranch hands who came to town on Saturday night. The Gillettes were right at home.[7]

Chester turned fourteen in Pendleton but the family was to stay less than six months. By November orders came for another change. It was only a short move, to Dayton, Washington just to the northeast.[8] In many ways Dayton was like the old days in Helena, Montana. There was farming, some ranching and in the mountains, mining. But the heyday of growth had been reached some fifteen years before. Mining had declined and the town's importance as a stagecoach hub disappeared with the coming of the railroads. Wheat farming in the semi-arid region was taking its first steps toward becoming a commercial enterprise. The Salvation Army had to contend with a stable, almost sleepy farm market town. Yet the Gillettes were to stay here for an entire year—a luxury in the move-about Salvation Army.[9]

The year 1898 was a slow one for the family. The Army ran a giant contest encouraging its members to sell subscriptions to the *War Cry*, the Salvation Army weekly. Each week the *War Cry* published the current standings by division, by corps and even by individual. Captain F. Gillette put together 42 points early in the campaign, but by summer when the national leaders had heady totals exceeding 300 points, Frank languished at 55 and never went higher. One suspects that he had pushed sales in Dayton as far as they would ever go.[10]

Whatever the reason for the unusually long stay in Dayton, it came to an abrupt halt in October of 1898, only a month short of the normal transfer time. For that one month the Gillettes were assigned to North Yakima (now Yakima) in Washington. The next assignment was in Portland, Oregon, a sizeable city and an old one in the Pacific Northwest. It seemed as if the Gillettes had put the small towns behind them, for Portland was certainly the most prestigious assignment in the division.[11]

Yet something was wrong. The tenure at Portland lasted only until spring when the Gillettes resigned from the Salvation Army. The resignation came in April but the reason behind it is a mystery. One might speculate that Frank Gillette's health had begun to decline, for in the years to follow he is often represented as a man of weak constitution.[12]

But there is a strong suspicion that personality may have played a part in the estrangement, for after a month the Gillettes were reinstated as captains, but this time they were in the neighboring California-Arizona division. Here they were assigned to one of the most distant posts, Laramie, Wyoming. The trip was long and the town was small, but it was fertile territory for the good fight.

Laramie was overshadowed by its more flamboyant cousin, Cheyenne, but when the Gillette family arrived in the summer of 1899 it still cherished a frontier reputation. It had once been a construction town at the end of the railroad and in its day it had known railroad boomers, Indians, range wars, cowboys and miners. Young Chester must have been delighted.

Ladies of the evening worked daylight shifts and the bars were both numerous and large. Many customers could remember the violence of the "old days" and newcomers from the East weren't sure that it was completely in the past.

Yet Laramie, of all the Wyoming cities, showed promise. The University of Wyoming opened here even before statehood was granted. The city relished music and drama and traveling companies played its theaters regularly. Temperance groups abounded and had begun to make some small headway in the realm of Sunday closings. It was a likely location for the Gillettes.[13] Chester spent most of his seventeenth year in Laramie, and the family was not transferred until May of 1900.

When transfer did come it was to Chico, California—another long trip back across the mountains. But it was a different West than they had known in Washington and Oregon. Chico is not in the cool coast range, but in California's central valley, some eighty miles north of Sacramento. Summers are long and arrogantly hot. Spokane and Dayton, though hot and dry, had been mere training camps when compared to the summers of the Sacramento Valley.[14]

The Gillettes never had the opportunity to spend a cool season in Chico. By the end of August they had been ordered on again— this time to Hawaii. A posting to the Hawaiian Islands was a mixed blessing. The *War Cry* often represented the islands as exotic with strange flowers, tropical trees, beautiful mountains and a population ripe for conversion.

But the *War Cry* also dropped dark hints about isolation, malnutrition and disease. More than one Salvation Army officer or wife returned to the mainland as a convalescent and it was difficult to determine whether the illness was related to the environment.

But distance and territorial status were old stuff to the Gillette family. A note in the *War Cry* told of their impending transfer:

Captain and Mrs. Gilette [sic] who made such a gallant fight in California are spoken of for far and fair Hawaii.[15]

In due time Frank Gillette led his wife and four children on board the SS China and left San Francisco for Honolulu.[16] It was quite an education. Chester was thoroughly seasick. They arrived in September of 1900 and took a local boat to the "Big Island" of Hawaii.

They were assigned to Hilo, the seaport city on the eastern side of Hawaii, but before long they were sent inland to the little village of Mountain View. Mountain View is located on the Mamalahoa highway that runs from Hilo to the Kilauea Crater, and the Gillettes found themselves twenty four miles up the road on the flanks of Mauna Loa. Mauna Loa is the dominant sight on Hawaii. In reality it *is* Hawaii for the island, large as it is, is only the top of this giant volcano that rises from the ocean bottom.

Unlike Mount Hood, Mount Ranier or Mount St. Helens, which explode from their dormancy to emit cinders and gas clouds, the Hawaiian volcanos push out great quantities of hot lava which cool while flowing down the mountain slopes to make new layers of dark, lava rock. On exposure to the atmosphere this rock turns to rich soil.

Along the Mamalahoa highway these elements are most impressive. The Gillettes had never before lived in a place where there was no winter, but here the temperature varies only slightly throughout the year. Even more mind-boggling is the rain. Nearly two hundred inches a year fall on Mountain View. In March, alone, the local residents expect about twenty inches! Having come from the semi-arid region of eastern Washington where the entire year's precipitation measures less than twenty inches, Chester must have been amazed.

The great rainfall combined with the warm temperatures quickly breaks the lava down into soil. The original vegetation here was an extensive rain forest, but along the road to Hilo the nineteenth century settlers had begun clearing the forest in order to establish plantations. The crop was sugar cane and the laborers were immigrants. The Salvation Army was interested in the latter.

The family faced a problem. The children were growing older and their education had suffered from the constant moving. Chester, particularly, needed something more than the primary schools that each community offered. The resources of a Salvation Army family did not ordinarily allow for expensive boarding schools but the Gillettes sought alternatives. There was Horace Gillette of Cortland (Frank's brother), as well as the elderly but wealthy Dr. Warner who had encouraged Chester's Aunt Carrie and Uncle Ellsworth to attend Oberlin's preparatory division a generation earlier.

In the winter of 1900–1901 the family arranged for Chester's entry into Oberlin's academy, as the preparatory division was now called. No doubt the parents had hopes that Chester would attend the college, but first it was necessary to finish the equivalent of a high school education and Chester's rather checkered background in a dozen different schools made it difficult to place him. Still, he was accepted. The presence of Dr. Warner on the board of trustees of Oberlin College did no harm at all.[17]

In the summer of 1901 Chester packed his belongings and prepared to leave Hawaii. At the age of eighteen he sailed for the mainland and left Salvation Army life forever. By September he had reached Ohio and lodged himself in a rooming house on East Lorain Street in the small college town of Oberlin. Oberlin College had established for itself a fine name in the nineteenth century and its young academy students were proud of their association with the older students at the college.

The Academy head, Professor Peck, placed Chester in the junior middle class, roughly equivalent to the modern high school sophomore.* His courses included Latin, History, English, Algebra

---

*The four years in the academy were called: Junior, Junior Middle, Middle and Senior.

and Bible, a rather typical program for the time and place. Classes met as frequently as five days a week (Latin and English) or as little as once a week (Bible).[18]

It was necessary for Chester to do some rapid catching up in Latin in order to place him in Latin IV with the rest of the class. His poorest grades were in English, but as the year went on he showed slow improvement. If he was not an outstanding student during the first year he was, at least, a consistent one. He did change rooming houses in the spring, moving to a house on West College Street.

Chester did not return to Hawaii at the end of the year. Instead, he traveled to Cortland and worked for his uncle, Horace, in the old wooden skirt factory.[19] Horace Gillette may have sponsored Chester at Oberlin and no doubt offered Chester a chance to work for some of his expenses. It was the first time Chester could remember being so far east and the first time he had visited the county where his father had been born.

In 1902 Chester's parents indulged in a long period of soul searching. It was never clear whether they lost their loyalty to the Salvation Army or were overwhelmed by a stronger force, but

The house on West College Street, Oberlin,
where Chester had a room.

49

during that year they resigned and left the Salvation Army and Hawaii.

The attraction was John Alexander Dowie. Dowie had burst forth on the American religious scene during the Chicago World's Fair in 1893. He was a faith healer who had formed his own church and like many a cult leader of the previous century, his own religion. He presented himself as the reincarnation of Elijah, or Elijah the second. The new religion was strewn with restrictive rules including a ban on tobacco, liquor, pork, medicine and medical practice. The church was fundamental in the extreme and called itself the Christian Catholic Apostolic Church in Zion.[20]

Dowie did more than establish a religion on paper or collect a congregation. In 1901 he built a community on the shores of Lake Michigan north of Chicago and called it Zion City. Here the exemplary life could be lived without the distractions and temptations of the outside world. Indeed, the community was shielded by a series of "blue laws" that made the little city something of a theocracy. Frank and Louise Gillette were drawn to the new sect like moths to a flame. By late 1902 they were among the faithful and living in Zion City, Illinois.

In September Chester returned to Oberlin and took a room on West Lorain. His relatives may have chosen Oberlin for its evangelical traditions, but a subtle change had crept over the college since Civil War times. It had become as interested in the mortal man as in the soul and some would charge that Oberlin had abandoned its religious duties altogether. In light of the weekly bible classes that remained in the curriculum, this may have been overstating it a bit. Still, Chester was living in a slightly more worldly society than his parents suspected.

He began the second year with only three academic courses and appears to have evaded Bible class altogether. It returned to his schedule during the second term but Chester's second year was a poor one. Bible class was bad and his English grades went down.* By the spring term he was carrying only two academic courses.[21] He had learned a great deal about college towns and rooming house life, but Chester was no scholar.

When Chester went home in the summer of 1903 it was to Zion

---

*Grades ran from zero to five with three as the passing mark. Chester's first year marks were better than four but in his second year he barely managed a three.

Chester, shown here with his hand on the basketball, evidently played with the preparatory division team during his time at Oberlin. The '08 on the basketball indicates that Chester would have been in the class of 1908 at Oberlin had he finished and gone on to the college division.

City, but he was soon on the road as a book salesman. His account of the year's work at Oberlin must have been overly vague for in late summer Louise Gillette wrote to Professor Peck seeking a clarification of her son's status:

Chester has been home for a short time this summer and is rather doubtful about going back next fall, as he undertook canvassing this summer and had an unsaleable book and poor territory. In consequence the whole summer has gone with little to show for it.

He is quite anxious to graduate from the academy and we would like to have him.

Did Mrs. Warner say anything to you about helping him next year? My brother-in-law Mr. N. H. Gillette of Cortland writes that she told him that she expected to help him. He bought a suit of clothes and books the past term for which he still owes in Oberlin. I suppose if you had not been away the latter part of the term he could have found out about this matter.

We received no report of Chester's work for the past term. Has he been doing his best in his school work?

He has been working in the harvest fields in S. Dakota for three weeks past.

    May God bless you in your good work for Him.

Yours in His service
L. M. Gillette[22]

    The letter sheds more light on Louise than on her son. She was, first of all, an avowed servant of the Lord. Moreover, she was an apologist for her son. Lastly, she tended to excuse Chester's actions by shifting responsibility to the shoulders of her audience. These characteristics would surface many times in the years to come.

    Chester did *not* return to Oberlin that fall, but remained in Zion City. He finally secured a position as a brakeman on the Chicago and Northwestern Railroad working out of Chicago. Sometime during 1904 Horace Gillette chanced to visit Chicago and met Chester again. There was talk about Chester's going to Cortland to work, but no firm plans were made.[23]

    But Chester must have thought about his uncle's offer many times that year for in the spring of 1905 he left Chicago. By the beginning of April he had arrived at his uncle's house in Cortland. Once again, Chester was starting a new life.[24] He left behind him an enviable record of travel. (See map on page 42.)

    Whether or not he was conscious of it, Chester was repeating Horace's own past as the boy from the West who worked his way up through an uncle's business in the industrial East—another Horatio Alger!

    But Chester lacked Horace's steady, conservative attention to detail and his commitment to hard work. Horace's favorite office motto, posted frequently in the factory, was "Stick to it." Chester, in spite of his dashing exterior, stuck to very little. In fact, he had the beginnings of a very proper inferiority complex. Shortly after arriving in Cortland he had occasion to relate a prank from his past:

> . . .reminds me of a mince pie that I tried very hard to dispose of without the others' knowledge. I made a failure of that as I do of most things.[25]

    It was not clear whether Chester was drawing a curtain on one era or opening one on another.

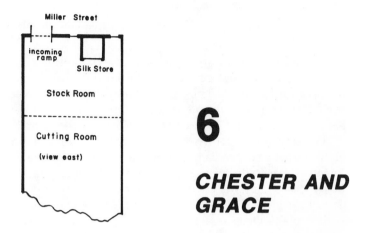

Miller Street

incoming ramp

Silk Store

Stock Room

Cutting Room

(view east)

6

CHESTER AND GRACE

Chester stepped off the south-bound train from Syracuse on a spring day in 1905 and sought out his uncle, Horace Gillette. Horace was surprised for he was not expecting his nephew. Nevertheless, Chester was taken to the house and a job was arranged in the factory working in the stockroom. His salary was set at ten dollars a week and remained at that level for the rest of his stay.[1]

The local newspaper duly noted his arrival and employment, commenting that Chester was staying with his uncle on West Court Street.[2] Chester was—but not for long. He was given to understand that he was to take lodgings of his own in the city and he proceeded to do just that. He may have indulged in a small bit of self pity at this point, for his two slightly younger cousins were full members of the Court Street household.

Harold, Horace's own son, had good reason to live in the house, but Leslie may have been a different matter in Chester's eyes. The little known nephew from Montana was in many ways much like Chester, but he lived with the Gillettes like a son and held an office in the company.[3]

Chester was strictly an inner page item in the Cortland daily. He could, after all, arrive in Cortland only once. The front pages were filled with Teddy Roosevelt and his vacation trip to the Southwest, with German sabre rattling in Morocco, and with the Russians. At that moment the Russian fleet was inching its way toward an engagement with the Japanese and world watchers followed its every movement with interest.

This home on Wheeler Avenue, the former Wheeler farm house, was where Grace roomed from the time her sister left Cortland until June of 1906.

But Chester was no world watcher. He had never pretended to be an avid reader and at this point in his life he was more interested in notices of "Room to Let," the impending arrival of the season's first circus, and in the acquisition of a bicycle. During most of his stay in Cortland Chester's travel was plebeian. His Uncle Horace and his cousin, Harold, experimented with the new and noisy motor car, but Chester rode his "wheel."

Once in a rooming house Chester was on his own. In many ways it was like Oberlin. He lived by himself and barring restrictions imposed by his landlady, came and went when he chose. (As in Oberlin, he changed rooms frequently.) By summer he was familiar with most of the streets in the small city and with the villages that lay just beyond. Horace made occasional suggestions, perhaps seeing himself in his young nephew. Chester seldom solicited advice, but in one respect he followed his uncle's example closely. He joined the Presbyterian Church and sat each Sunday with the town's finest families.

He might have sought acquaintances from among the young men and women of the Normal School, but by the time Chester had settled into his new life the school year had ended and the Normal

This double house (#17½ on the left) on East Main Street was Chester's last address in Cortland. His room was the last on the left on the second floor.

students had gone home for the summer. Chester turned to outdoor activity. On weekends he peddled his bicycle around the city and to nearby towns.

On weekdays he rode to work, parking his bike in the shed that had been built for that purpose several years before. It was the only part of the factory that had escaped the fire of 1904. Chester found the new factory to be an unlovely box-like structure with three floors and an attic. (He had worked in the old factory when he spent his summer vacation in Cortland in 1902). The building was remarkable for its many windows. When designed it was hoped that they would be thrown open during the lunch hour in order to air the building. No one would be able to call the Gillette factory a sweat shop!

The main floor was the middle of the three principal levels and was entered by office staff and guests by way of a covered stoop on the south side. Nine steps took the customer up to the entrance. Inside, the entire southeastern corner was taken up by executive offices and in the extreme southeast corner was Horace's own office. His desk sat on the opposite side of the wall from the building's cornerstone. In the next cubicle north was a ten foot square walk-in vault for company papers. Since the vault was windowless there was one gap in the otherwise regular pattern of windows that faced Miller street.[4]

But Chester did not work on the main floor. He was assigned to the stock room where parts and material were received and stored until needed in the cutting room.[5] All of this activity went on in the sunken first floor rooms of the factory. The floor was only partially below ground level, thus it was not a true basement, but its windows, which started at grade level, were smaller than those of the upper floors.

The receiving and store rooms were located across the east side of this floor. There was access to Miller street for deliveries. There was also ready access to the cutting room in the western end of the same floor.[6]

It was here that Chester found Grace Brown working. She cut sections of skirt material from bolts of cloth which were drawn from the stockroom. Some of the finer silks were stored in a fireproof vault that was a lower extension of the records vault near Mr. Gillette's office. The cut pieces that left Grace's table went on an endless chain to the third floor where machine operators sewed them into completed garments.

Chester was quite taken with the young Chenango County girl who had never been a hundred miles from home. She was tiny—only five feet high—and she barely weighed one hundred pounds. Her face was too long and narrow to be called pretty but Chester found her attractive. He discovered excuses to visit her table and what started as small talk soon grew into friendship. The country girl and the boy from the West paired off.[7]

During the summer Chester called on Grace in the evenings. The walk to Fifth Avenue was a short one, for Grace lived only a few blocks beyond the factory. The street was short and the house was small. Chester managed to come two and three times a week and sat with Grace in the front parlor.

Ada, Grace's married sister, was quite interested in the young man who had suddenly started keeping company with her younger sister. She talked at length with Chester about his long and round-about journey through the West. But she appears not to have objected to Chester's presence. Possibly there was magic in the Gillette name and the knowledge that Chester was a nephew of the factory owner. Horace was, after all, a man of substance in the community.[8]

Chester seemed to be elated with his new relationship. He called Grace "Billy," and when she returned home for a two week visit in the fall he wrote long letters to South Otselic. Whether they were written in earnest or in an attempt to overwhelm an innocent young girl will never be known, but Chester "poured it on:"

> I am glad to hear you are having such a fine time because you wont [sic] be lonesome as I am. . .. You don't know how lonesome it is now, with less work for me to do, and nothing to do evenings. Last night I rode to Little York, and then went to bed. Sunday was the dullest day I have known in a long time. . .. Sunday I went to church three times [!], something I haven't done in a long time. . .. I went to bed about nine, but laid awake for nearly two hours thinking of everything, principally you. . .. Hurry back as you don't know how lonesome it is here.
>
> With Love,
Chester[9]

Chester had never excelled in writing and for him these words bordered on eloquence. There was even time for an apology or two:

> I know we were out awfully late, but we did the best we could under the circumstances. I shall never let it occur again if I can help it. . .. Dear, how I miss you, but not for the work you did. You always accuse me of that although you don't believe it.[10]

The misunderstandings mentioned in these lines refer to problems known only to Chester and Grace. Grace was prone to take Chester to task for statements and actions, but at this point in their relationship Chester tended to be contrite. He was out to make an impression.

In September of 1905 something happened which may have affected the entire story of Grace and Chester. Ada went home to South Otselic with her son, Robert. On returning to Cortland she left the child with his grandparents for an extended visit. What started as a holiday for a little boy ended in tragedy. Somewhere in the dangerous nooks and crannies of the house and barn little Robert blundered into a frightening accident. Dr. Crumb who had married Grace's former teacher, worked to save the child but the mishap proved fatal. By the time that Grace and Ada arrived from Cortland Robert was dead.

The family was grief stricken and Grace remained temporarily in South Otselic to help her mother and Ada. Chester, who had known Robert from his visits to the house on Fifth Avenue wrote a brief note of condolence:

Dear Billy,

It was with sadness and deep sorrow that I learned of your bereavement. It was a great surprise and shock to me as I did not understand your reason for going home so suddenly. I am very sorry for both you and your sister, and wish that I could in some way have lightened your sorrow. Please express my deep sorrow to your sister.

Ever your sincere friend,
Chester[11]

In their grief, the Hawleys left Cortland altogether and Grace no longer had a relative to live with. The solution was the rooming house at Mrs. Wheeler's and it was here that Chester continued to call during the winter. Carrie Wheeler became accustomed to seeing the young Gillette man call on her roomer at least twice a week but during the winter it was too cold to sit on the porch and Grace entertained her visitor in the parlor. Mrs. Wheeler was a very proper landlady but the solution may have been an imperfect one.[12]

At the factory Chester continued to wander away from the stockroom area to visit Grace's table. Theresa Harnischfeger, a forewoman in the cutting room, was the person who most often had to break up these tête-à-têtes. It was an awkward chore because Chester was not easily put down, yet it was necessary because Chester's attentions to Grace were disturbing the room. For Miss Harnischfeger it was a duty she could not ignore for Horace Gillette had expressly indicated that Chester was not to leave the stockroom.[13]

But Chester did not call on Grace every night, nor did he see her every weekend. There were other girls in the factory whom he saw occasionally, much to Billy's distress, and he soon discovered girls among the students at the Normal School. Chester's loyalty was far from total.

Yet he continued to see Grace as a matter of routine and the two young lovers maintained a slightly strained relationship. He continued to call her "Billy" and shared her joke about "Billy the Kid." Sometimes she was just "Kid."

In April of 1906 Grace left Cortland once more. Her sister, Ada, now living much closer to the Brown family was due to have another baby, and as usual Grace went home to help. Her absence gave Chester a bit more freedom of movement and caused a slightly greater strain on their fragile relationship.

Grace wrote Chester immediately on arriving home. Her letter was long and chatty and she described in detail the parties that had been arranged for her. If she overstressed the attention that her family and friends heaped on her it was probably an attempt to impress Chester:

> . . . we got home about 2 O'Clock. Mama is at Mrs. Hawley's and I am a little bit lonesome. We have had guests here all day and have engagements for every day and evening until next Tuesday. Say: I don't know as you remember, but the Alpha Deltas have their Club Public a week from Saturday night.* I thought you intended to go down there. If I come back Tuesday, you will come up Tuesday night, won't you dear?. . . I want you to write and tell me, dear, that you can come up Tuesday night. Of course I could stay until week from Sat. but I want to go to the Club Public. You let me have my way this time dear, and I won't never ask for my way again.[14]

When Grace spoke of Mrs. Hawley she was referring to her sister, Ada. To a modern reader this may seem like unnatural usage, but Chester had been quite proper during his visits to the house on Fifth Avenue and no doubt he had addressed Ada as Mrs. Hawley. And, too, it was a more formal era.

But there was nothing restrained about Grace's plea to meet the following week. Moreover she was most eager to attend the club outing in Cortland the next Saturday. Whether this stemmed from a real desire to visit a Normal School function, or to watch over Chester when *he* went to one is a matter of conjecture. Yet if Grace struggled too hard to keep Chester interested, she also pressed him too closely. In the same letter she said:

> . . . I hope you are satisfied and having what you call a good time now that you have succeeded in making me leave Cortland for a time. It makes me feel badly, dear, to think that you think I didn't know why you wanted me to come home. I know that I may be awfully green, but as you say, "I ain't no fool.". . . Please write me a long, cheery letter and tell me all about how you have not thought about me once or missed me at all and how you don't want me to come back and how you can't possibly come up until week from Sat. night if I do come back. . .[15]

There was a note of desperation in the girl's letter as she set out each item for him to contradict. Chester, however, was unimpressed by this sad little attempt at irony and snatched at the opportunity she

---

*Alpha Delta was Normal School sorority. Once a year the organization held an annual event open to the public—a club public.

held out. In a letter that was much more terse and cool than those of six months earlier he said:

> . . . I am too tired to write, but will do the best I can. I have been out one night this week, and yet I am tired out and am going to bed early. . . .. You had better decide to stay longer though, as I think it would be for your good. I could not possibly come up until Thursday night and possibly not until Friday so do not plan on it. As to the numerous accusations you make, they are all true, so perhaps I had better not come at all. In fact I think that would be better for both. Do not think I am saying this because I am tired but because I think it best. I hope you will feel better when you come back, but do not rush your work too hard because of it. Hoping you will understand my reasons for writing as I do, I remain
>
> Yours truly,
C[16]

Gone were the flowing words meant to impress a young woman. Chester was short and businesslike. He was playing out the role of the young man intent on escaping the confinements of a relationship. Chester was beginning to value his "fun" and fun meant other girls and other parties. He was rather like a boy who, in his first year of college, discovers that he does not want to "go steady" with his high school sweetheart after all.

Grace never had an opportunity to respond in writing. She returned to Cortland early as she had promised (or threatened), and her last letter crossed in the mails with Chester's abrupt note of dismissal. The letter was long and newsy with only a few allusions to her previous pique:

> My Dear Chester —
>   I won't have time to write you again before I come back so I will write you a few lines. . . I came down to breakfast about 9 O'Clock this morning and I heard my youngest sister crying. She had found her pet canary dead in his cage and her poor little heart was broken. We had a very grand funeral and she is feeling some better tonight.
>   I have looked for a letter from you. There were six on my plate when I came down for breakfast this morning but I was disappointed in not finding one from you. . . Are you lonesome without me? I have not had time to be lonesome, but I miss you very much and I shall be pleased to see you again. . . I know very nearly everything you have done since I came away. I mean by that that I have imagined what you've done. I was wondering today if you were in the basement or the stockroom. . . .. I hope to see you Tuesday night, anyhow, and I hope you will be pleased to see me. . . ..[17]

Grace was grasping at straws in making an appeal for Chester's affection. His tart response was already in the mail. Grace, in turn, may have relied on more than her imagination in cataloging Chester's actions. The letters on her plate were from friends in Cortland. Grace was quite aware of Chester's activities.

After her return to Cortland their confrontations were face to face, and there is no written record of how their little quarrels were patched up. But patched they were—for the time being at least—although Grace probably granted concessions to Chester.

Somewhere in the months after her return a new and ominous factor emerged. It had begun in the spring, probably just before her April trip to South Otselic. Now, in the aftermath of her vacation and the bickering with Chester came the first clues, the first slow fears, and then the frightening realization. Billy Brown was pregnant.[18]

7

FEAR AND DESPERATION

In 1906 a girl who was pregnant and unmarried had on her hands a monstrous problem. Little wonder that in those days (and for years to come) to say that a girl was "in trouble" meant that she was both unwed and expecting.

It is difficult to appreciate the predicament in which Grace was trapped. Should her problems become public knowledge she would be treated as a social outcast. With the threat of stigma hanging over her she could confide in no one; not her parents, who would feel outrage and hurt; not her companions of the factory who were too casual with secrets; not a counselor, for in that day there were none. There was, of course, the clergy but whether Grace dared to share her secret with a minister is doubtful and in any event he could offer as solutions, only prayer and marriage.

Grace may well have resorted to prayer, but marriage was more elusive. There is no indication that Chester offered. If Grace sought marriage as a way out, Chester failed to step into the breach and there was no spring wedding, or even a promise of one. Yet it is difficult to guess and impossible to know what went on between the two in the weeks after Grace's return to Cortland. No letters passed between them—at least none that have survived. Their conversations and quarrels were never public.

The blackout lasted until the middle of June and one can only speculate on their attempts to solve the problem. Abortion must have been among the topics they discussed, but abortion was unlawful in the public realm, and an anathema to the Church. There is no way of knowing whether the two young people even considered it, yet one thing is certain. Under today's law Grace could have, and probably would have, availed herself of the opportunity. Had she been able to do so this story would have ended in 1906, and Grace and Chester could have spent long, if unspectacular lives.

A few things are known about Chester and Grace during the months of May and early June. They were often seen by others although their conversations went unrecorded. On Decoration Day (Memorial Day) Chester went out, but not with Grace. By now there was no question of Grace's being pregnant nor that Chester was the father. Yet Chester spent the day with a friend, William Short, at Glen Haven on the south shore of Skaneateles Lake. The two young men took with them Georgia Hoag, Chester's second cousin, and Iva Dufree, a girl from the factory.[1]

That it was a callous act is self evident but coming as it did on the big weekend that opened the summer season made it seem even worse. To Grace it must have appeared as one more clue that Chester really did not care. This one event was the first of many doubts that began to plague little Billy Brown.

Had Chester abandoned Grace entirely her choices would have been more clear. She might have fled the city or denounced Chester publicly. But she continued to hope, and he continued to call, though not every night. On occasion he even took her out. One summer evening in mid-June Chester rented a horse and buggy and took Grace to Little York Lake.

At Raymond's he rented a rowboat and took Grace for a ride on the lake. They were gone less than an hour before coming in to the landing. As Mr. Raymond helped the two ashore, he noticed that the young woman was in tears.[2] Chester drove her away in the dark. He might have ridden to Little York more cheaply on the trolly, but the buggy offered more privacy and Chester seldom took Grace out in public.

Even as her pregnancy advanced, Chester alternated his attentions, finding time to accommodate Grace, girls in the factory, and newer girls from the Normal school. Late in June Josephine Patrick, a Normal student, drove up to the factory in a dog cart and asked for Chester.* He left the floor, walked outside, and chatted

---

*A dog cart was a small horse-drawn conveyance similar to an Irish jogging cart except that the seats faced forward and back. Originally, hunting dogs were kept beneath the rear seat.

with the visitor for a long time while Grace watched the door from her table. Chester returned to the stockroom and Grace followed him inside. When she finally came back to the cutting room she sat down at her table and cried uncontrollably.[3]

By the middle of June Grace decided to go home for another vacation. Informal holidays at home were common enough, although there were no paid vacations for workers in those days. Grace had already been home once during the previous autumn and again in April. Still, no one protested this new request.

Before leaving the factory Grace copied down descriptions of her favorite skirts. She, herself, was a poor seamstress but Maude Kenyon, now Maude Crumb, often helped out when Grace was home on vacation. Billy hoped to have new clothes made during her stay in South Otselic.

But if the trip home was routine, Grace struggled constantly to keep up appearances. She was concerned that her pregnancy was soon going to "show" and while a vacation with her family might avoid discovery in Cortland, it only jeopardized her secret at home. The trip would be but a temporary solution. She could buy some time with it but after that something had to happen.

Chester seemed to concur. Indeed, it may have been his own idea, but leaving Chester was tempting fate. While there are clues that the two planned to leave on a trip at the conclusion of her stay, there is no indication that Grace knew exactly what Chester had in mind. Every day at home would be one during which she would be completely reliant on Chester's ultimate arrival with a solution. The "vacation" in South Otselic promised to be an anxious rather than a happy one. Her only link with Chester would be by mail.

In any event, Chester and Grace sat in the dark on the porch of the Wheeler House on Saturday the sixteenth and talked until late in the evening.[4] Grace might well have left Cortland the next day except that the only train out on Sunday was the very early milk train. It was Monday before she went to the DL&W station and took the 10:05 a.m. train for Cincinnatus, the closest station to South Otselic.

She didn't feel well and the one-coach train was grimy and uncomfortable. The train stopped at five intermediate stations and was subject to flag stops at two more.[5] After seventeen miles and an hour and ten minutes she found herself on the platform at Cincinnatus. A relative was waiting with a team to drive the twelve miles home.

As Grace started home bad news arrived. Her sister was very ill and Grace sent her luggage on to the farmhouse while she rushed to her sister's home. Even while she plunged into this more unwelcome news came. A brother reported that her parents were planning to go away for the entire summer, taking Grace with them. This was alarming for she was given to understand that the trip would begin in a week and she was frightened that it would become impossible to meet Chester at the end of June.[6]

Yet if she remained with the family for another two months her condition would certainly become obvious. Little wonder that she wrote Chester that very night saying:

> I have often heard the saying, "It never rains but it pours", but I never knew what it meant until today. . . Everything worries me and I am so frightened, dear. . .[7]

Grasping for solutions, Grace reasoned that disaster could be avoided if Chester would come for her earlier than they had arranged. Already she was planning to have new clothes made prior to his arrival, and now she tried to cope with a shrinking timetable by having some dresses made up as soon as possible.

> It won't make any difference to you about your coming a few days earlier than you intended will it dear? It means so much to me. I will have my dresses made if I can and I will try and be very brave, dear. Perhaps you will never know what a task it was for me to come home, but we can't help things now, and we may as well act like human beings. I think, dear, I have done all I could do with the journey last month and everything. . .[8]

What journey, indeed? This is the first time either Chester or Grace speaks of a trip during the month of May. Where they went and how, and above all the reason for such travel is a mystery. Grace was worried, and this first letter to Chester betrays even more fear than she admitted to at the time:

> . . .You won't miss me as much on account of your work, but Oh dear—please write and tell me you will come for me before week from Saturday. I will come straight back to C— if you don't come before then . . . I wish I could have had Ella and Maud out here next week, but Mama won't be home so I can't have them. . .* This is a horrible letter but I can't write a better one, I am so blue.
>
> Lovingly,
> Your G. M. B.[9]

---

*Ella Melvin and Maud Odell were friends of Grace who worked in the factory.

That first night Grace stayed at her sister's house and her father posted the letter next day. But more trouble arrived, this time from Cortland. Grace had friends at the factory (probably Maud and Ella) who were more than eager to watch over Chester's activities. One such report arrived in Tuesday's mail. Grace wrote again that very night. The full impact of her isolation from Chester and her terrible dependence on him were just beginning to make themselves felt.

> My Dear Chester—I am just ready for bed and am so ill I could not help writing you. I never came down this morning until nearly 8 O'Clock and I fainted about 10 O'Clock and stayed in bed until nearly noon. This afternoon my brother brought me a letter from one of the girls, and after I read the letter I fainted again. Chester, I came home because I thought I could trust you. I don't think now I will be here after next Friday. This girl wrote me that you seemed to be having an awfully good time and she guessed my coming home had done you good, for you had not seemed so cheerful in weeks. She also said that you spend most of your time with that detestable Grace Hill.[10]

Unlike Josephine Patrick who was a Normal School student, Grace Hill was a skirtmaker who lived on Fitz Avenue (now West Main Street), and she was not one of Grace's favorite people. Once again Grace found that fainting was a powerful idea, but this time it was a frightening one. Whether Chester saw it that way is another matter. Grace alternated between anger and fear—fear that Chester would not come:

> I have been very brave since I came home but tonight I am very discouraged. Papa was frightened today and insists on having the doctor up in the morning. I presume you won't think you can come for me when I asked you to. . .[11]

Anger and fear were a powerful combination and as she wrote Grace slipped into despair:

> Chester, if I could only die. I know how you feel about the affair and I wish for your sake you need not be troubled. If I die I hope then you can be happy. I hope I can die. . . Oh, dear, please come and take me away. You won't ever know how much I wish you would come. Chester I do want you to have a good time now and I won't be cross. I think when I see you, dear, I shall be so glad I can't live. I hope you will be glad to see me. Go where you want to dear, and don't be angry with me. I want you tonight and I am so blue.
>
> Lovingly,
The Kid

P.S. Write often, please.[12]

Unfortunately Grace vacillated between scolding Chester and forgiving him. Indeed, in her last lines she almost gave Chester her blessing, knowing perhaps, that he would go in any event.

Chester's reply crossed in the mail with Grace's Tuesday letter and he conveniently avoided any reference to his outside activities. Rather, he attempted to calm the girl in her first area of concern— her parents' plans for the summer:

Dear Grace:
Please excuse paper and pencil, as I am not writing this at home and have nothing else here. I received your letter last night and was just a little surprised although I thought you would be discouraged. Don't worry so much and think less about how you feel and have a good time. Your trip with your father and mother ought not to make any difference as you can go from where ever they are at any time. . . The girls are planning on their trip and will be disappointed when they learn they cannot go. I cannot get away before the 7th or 8th. . . I also think you should go with your parents and write while with them and we can make arrangements then.

Yours lovingly,
C[13]

Chester could well afford to tell Grace "Not to worry." He was not the one who was pregnant. Still, he held out the promise of meeting Grace during the summer, even if she should leave on a family trip. But in spite of the tender closing Chester was short and to the point. If he intended to allay Grace's fears he failed.

In the weeks that followed their letters kept to the same, familiar path. She pleaded and scolded, while Chester was careful and circumspect. For every letter Chester wrote Grace mailed three. His were short. Hers were long and her pleas became a litany.

By the end of the first week Grace was fretting over Chester's failure to write. It was becoming evident that he wasn't writing frequently at all:

My Dear Chester—
I am just wild because I don't get a letter from you. If you wrote me Tues. night and posted it Wed. morning there isn't any reason why I shouldn't get it. Are you sure you addressed the letter right? . . . You will get this Monday sometime. Now please write to me Monday night and post it Tuesday morning, and I will get it, or ought to, Wednesday morning. . . Please write me or I shall go crazy. Be a good Kid and God bless you,

Lovingly,
"the Kid"

P.S. — I am crying[14]

No sooner had she mailed this than Chester's abrupt reply arrived. This wasn't at all what Grace was looking for and that night she began in a very tart vein indeed:

> I was glad to hear from you and surprised as well. I thought you would rather have my letters affectionate, but yours was so businesslike that I have come to the conclusion that you wish mine to be that way. . . I think—pardon me—that I understand my position and that it is rather unnecessary for you to be so frightfully frank in making me see it. . .[15]

Then Grace began to warm up to the topic that bothered her most—Chester's extracurricular activities. There was even a bit of threat buried in the letter:

> The girls write me that you are planning on another trip for the Fourth of July. They never wrote me how they knew of it, perhaps you told them. Is that the reason you cannot come before the seventh or eighth? Chester, I didn't mind being snubbed and put aside Decoration Day for the other girls, but I do mind it the Fourth. I have always had to be put aside for other girls on such occasions and presume it will always be that way. This is the truth, isn't it? . . . I don't care the least only I think the girl would feel highly edified if she knew you were going away so soon, don't you? . . . I think I shall be back the last of this week. [!] I can't tell just when. That depends on when my dresses are done. I won't interfere with any of your plans. . .[16]

There is a slight hint here that Chester had made their upcoming trip sound like something permanent, possibly a move to another life away from Cortland. A few lines later the suggestion is repeated:

> My whole life is ruined and in a measure yours is too. Of course it's worse for me than for you, but the world and you, too, may think that I am the one to blame, but somehow I can't—just simply can't think I am, Chester. I said no so many times, dear. . .[17]

Grace was beginning to apply pressure. Her threat to return to Cortland was not part of Chester's plan. He wanted to meet her in South Otselic or in any town in which the Browns vacationed. (The parents' trip had already been delayed, probably by her sister's illness.) After that would come Grace's trip, a trip on which she would take her trunk and new dresses. A return to Cortland at this point sounded like a threat to expose her condition.

She had already found a more serious way of taking Chester to task. In the absence of letters she had gone to the South Otselic hotel where there was a telephone booth. From this she placed a call to the skirt factory in Cortland and asked for Chester.[18] The operator called him from the stockroom and it was necessary to talk where others could hear.[19]

The conversation was stormy but she succeeded. She had his complete attention. Chester wrote immediately and then another letter—longer, chattier and almost conciliatory in tone. After a few sentences of idle chatter he came directly to the point:

> Perhaps I wrote too harshly Friday about your telephoning and your worry but it was entirely unnecessary and not at all satisfactory because I couldn't say what I wanted to. Don't do such a foolish thing again. . .[20]

Grace had unwittingly touched a raw nerve. On the other hand she may have known exactly what she was doing. One thing Chester could not risk at that point in time was a public argument with Grace. Disclosure of their relationship would create difficulties with his employer who had made it clear that Chester was not to hang around the cutting tables. It caused him embarrassment in the work spaces where (in spite of the rule) he was prone to chat with the other girls. Moreover, word might reach some of the middle class girls of the town among whom he had begun to find friends.

He was most irritated by the stream of information that was steadily trickling back to Grace from her friends in the factory and he singled them out in a postscript:

> P.S. The girl that wrote all that to you later told me about it and said she stretched things in order to get you to believe them. She kindly told me of the things she had told you and said you were foolish to believe me rather than her but that you always did. Of course if you are going to believe her I might as well not say anything and see what you think then. The things you wrote were not so, at least some of them were not, and especially those G. H. [Billy's nemesis, Grace Hill?] said. She isn't here half the time so that would stop a great deal even tho I did do what E [Ella Melvin] says. Please forgive anything harsh I have said and dont [sic] worry for two weeks.
>
> Lovingly,
C[21]

Now one can understand Chester's low grades in English four years earlier! Still, he made his point even if he lacked eloquence. He forced Grace to take either his word or that of the girls. But Grace was already feeling regret for bringing up the subject and after

Chester's second letter she again attempted to smooth over the affair of Chester's activities:

> I hope you got my letter asking your forgiveness for that horrid letter I wrote . . . Chester, dear, I hope you will have an awfully nice time the 4th. Really, dear, I don't care where you go or who you go with if you only come on the 7th. You are so fond of boating and the water why don't you go on a trip that will take you to some lake? I was cross and ill when I wrote about it before, but really I don't mind the least bit and I hope you will go. . .[22]

By her own description Grace was thin and ashen. She cried much of the time and was ill daily. Whether this stemmed from pregnancy and fear, or was merely an imaginative invention to gain Chester's sympathy will never be known, but her letters turned dark and morose.

> Oh! dear, dear, dear! I can't see anything but just trouble. What if I should not be able to travel. There are so many things to think about. If I had the strength, dear, I do believe I should walk to the river and throw myself in. . . You would smile if you knew how I am trying to get strong, for I don't care how rough my life is after next Saturday. I think I could carry packs like women peddlers, but I shall certainly die if you don't come. . .[23]

Chester's third letter was written just before the Fourth of July and dealt with the previous weekend. It was abrupt, starting with "Dear Kid—" and ended simply with "C". In it he described his weekend experiences:

> . . . Saturday I went up to the lake Little York Lake and am so burned tonight I cannot wear a collar or coat. We went out in the canoe and to two other lakes, and, although the canoe was heavy to carry, we had a good time but I got my arms awfully burned. . .[24]

Chester was dealing with safe subjects here. Grace, however, after reacting with pleasure to getting one of his rare letters, couldn't resist commenting on his weekend of boating:

> I do wish you could read some of the letters from the girls. It is no wonder I write blue letters. I don't believe what they say now, dear. I wish you could have read one letter, giving an account of your trip to the lake. Of course I had received your letter telling me about it so I did not believe the other one, but it was so different. Of course you boys all had girls and all that stuff and nonsense. I was awfully glad I had your letter first though. . .[25]

It was Chester's word against the girls', yet Grace had little choice but to believe Chester. At the moment she had more to worry about than Chester's weekend gambolings. During the two weeks that had passed since her departure he had been extremely vague about their future plans. He hadn't improved much when he wrote to Grace:

> I really have no plans beyond that, as I do not know how much money I can get or anything about the country. If you have any suggestions to make I wish you would and also just when and where you can meet me. I have said nothing more about going away but shall simply leave Sunday July 8th ... As for my plans for the Fourth I have made none as the only two girls I could get to go with me have made other arrangements because I didn't ask them until Saturday and to-day, so that some one is mistaken. . . [26]

Chester's casual attitude toward their plans to meet frightened the girl. By this time she was almost beyond worrying about his blatant relationships with other girls. (He had treated his lack of a holiday date almost as a virtue.) Grace wanted only a firm date and place where they could meet. She dwelt upon it.

> ... You have been at Little York for two Sun. now haven't you? I'm very glad you had a nice time. You did not say if there were any girls in this last trip. In your last letter you said you could get away the 7th or at least you would, and in tonight's letter you will meet me Mon. I expect any time to hear you can't come for a week or two yet. I am awfully sorry but I have planned on Sat. and I shall be in Cortland that night unless you meet me . . .. I was boiling mad when I found you did not want to come until Monday, Dear, but now if you want things that way you can have them. . .[27]

As usual Grace relented and accepted Chester's plans, including the Monday meeting. On the very day that her letter was mailed Chester took Harriet Benedict to dinner at Little York and played games with the Raymond House register. At that point in time Grace had only a sketchy plan to meet Chester on the following Monday. When the Fourth was over she wrote her last letter. The long rambling paragraphs were, in effect, her farewell to home and family:

My Dear Chester:
    I am curled up by the kitchen fire and you would shout if you could see me. Every one else is in bed. The girls came up and we shot off the last firecrackers. Our lawn looks about as green as the Cortland House corner. I will tell you all about my Fourth when I see you. I hope you had a nice time. This is the last letter I can write, dear. I feel

72

as though you were not coming. Perhaps that is not right, but I can't help feeling that I am never going to see you again. How I wish this was Monday. I am going down to stay with Maude next Sunday night, dear, and then go to DeRuyter the next morning and will get there about 10 O'Clock. If you take the 9:45 train from the Lehigh there you will get here about 11. I am sorry I could not go to Hamilton, dear, but papa and mamma did not want me to go and there are so many things I have had to work hard for in the last two weeks. They think I am just going out there to DeRuyter for a visit. Now, dear, when I get there I will go at once to the hotel and I don't think I will see any of the people.* If I do and they ask me to come to the house, I will say something so they won't mistrust anything. Tell them we were to meet there to go to a funeral or a wedding in some town further along. Awfully sorry, but we were invited to come and so I had to cut my vacation a little short and go. Will that be all O.K. dear? Maybe that won't be just what I will say but don't worry about anything for I shall manage somehow. Only I want you to come in the morning for I have had to make—you don't know how many plans to fit your last letter—in order to meet you Monday. I dislike waiting until Monday, but now that we have to, I don't think it anything only fair that you would come Monday morning. But dear, you must see the necessity yourself of getting there and not making me wait. If you dislike the idea of coming Monday morning and can get a train up there Sunday, you can come up Sunday night and be there to meet me. Perhaps that would be the best way. All I care is that I don't want to wait there all day or half a day. I think there is a train that leaves the Lehigh at six something Sunday night. I don't know what I would do if you were not there or did not come. I am about crazy now.

I have been bidding goodby to some places today. There are so many nooks, dear, and all of them so dear to me. I have lived here nearly all my life. First I said good by to the spring house with its great masses of green moss, then the apple tree where we had our playhouse; then the "beehive" a cute little house in the orchard, and of course all the neighbors that have mended my dresses from a little tot up, to save me from a threshing I really deserved.

Oh, dear, you don't realize what all of this means to me. I know I shall never see any of them again, and mamma! Great heavens how I love mamma! I don't know what I shall do without her. She is never cross and she always helps me so much. Sometimes I think if I could tell mamma, but I can't. She has trouble enough as it is and I couldn't break her heart like that. If I come back dead, perhaps if she does know, she won't be angry with me. I will never be happy again, dear. I wish I could die. You will never know what you have made me suffer,

---

*Grace had relatives in DeRuyter.

dear. I miss you and I want to see you but I wish I could die. I am going to bed now, dear. Please come and don't let me wait there. It is for both of us to be there. If you have made plans for something Sunday night you must come Monday morning.

Please think, dear, that I had to give up a whole summer's pleasure and you surely will be brave enough to give up one evening for me. I shall expect and look for you on Monday forenoon.

Heaven bless you till then. Lovingly and with kisses.

The Kid

I will go right to the Tabor House and you come for me there. I wish you would come up Sunday night so as to be there, and sweetheart, I think it would be easier for you. Please come up Sunday night dear.[28]

8

JOURNEY TO DISASTER

Chester did come.

Some of his plans were vague, and no doubt the specific meeting was arranged through a letter that never became public. At any rate the two agreed to meet in the little village of DeRuyter on Monday the 9th and each began to prepare for the coming trip.

FRIDAY

Chester finished his work at the factory on Friday but not before checking with Ella Hoag (Horace's cousin and the paymistress) to see if he could draw twenty dollars in pay. He could not. She pointed out that she could not pay against future wages. His weekly paycheck of ten dollars was all that he could collect on that particular Friday.[1] For a young man about to embark on a major trip Chester enjoyed very limited resources, and he now sought other avenues.

SATURDAY

He went to his uncle's house on Saturday night to seek help. He asked Mr. Gillette if he had a mileage book he might use.* Horace was aware of Chester's trip (but not its purpose) and had no objections. However, he had no mileage book and lent Chester money with which to buy one.[2] Chester would be able to leave on

---

*A mileage book was a kind of open ticket with no destination listed. The conductor merely punched out the number of miles used.

The Lehigh Valley Railroad Station in Cortland at the turn of the century. It was from here that Chester left Cortland for the last time.

the weekend with at least one week's pay and railroad transportation guaranteed.

SUNDAY

On Sunday Chester and Grace both made final preparations for the trip. Chester went to the Presbyterian Church as usual, and after church he talked at length with his uncle about his vacation. He left Horace with the impression that he was still torn between the Thousand Islands and the Adirondacks.[3]

Now it was necessary for Chester to find an acquaintance to substitute for him the following Sunday. Chester was either an organ pumper or an usher (both roles were described in later years by local churchgoers) and he carefully made sure that he was "covered" for the following week. If Chester was leaving Cortland, he gave every indication that he intended to return.

It was late afternoon when Grace left the farm outside South Otselic. She was to meet Chester in DeRuyter the following morning, but there was no train service in South Otselic and connections to DeRuyter were awkward. There was, however, an early "stage" or horse-drawn conveyance that left South Otselic in

The Tabor House Hotel in DeRuyter where Chester met Grace on the morning of July 9th.

the morning. After telling her family that she was returning to Cortland by way of DeRuyter, Grace took her belongings to Maude Crumb's house in the village. Here she could stay the night and be on hand for the ride to DeRuyter next day.[4]

Chester, too, started out on Sunday night. Grace had pressed him to take the night train to DeRuyter so that he would be there when she arrived on Monday morning. He dropped off the train at 8:10 on Sunday night.

At 8:30 Chester appeared at the Tabor House, a hotel located a half mile from the station. He had a suitcase with a tennis racket strapped to the side, and carried an umbrella. If Chester was trying to blend into the background he failed, for the tennis racket drew the attention of everyone who saw him in the little town of DeRuyter.[5]

Chester did not seek a room immediately, although he was seen by the wife of the hotel proprietor. A reporter later quoted the proprietor himself as saying that Chester had approached him at this time asking for directions to South Otselic and a rig to get there. According to the story the hotel owner refused when he heard that Chester's objective was the Brown farm, for it was an even greater distance than the village of South Otselic.[6]

It was an unlikely story for by 8:30 darkness was rapidly approaching and Chester would have been a poor risk to guide a horse and buggy over strange roads in the dark. Still, Chester did leave the hotel and remained away until nearly eleven o'clock. What he did during those two hours is a mystery, but the time was insufficient for a trip to South Otselic, even in daylight.

At about ten minutes to eleven Chester reappeared with his suitcase and tennis racket. The hotel clerk, who doubled as bartender, gave him the register to sign and placed him in room five. He then wrote down a call for 7:30 a.m. and showed Chester to the room. Chester was alone that night, yet he registered in the hotel in a strange manner. He signed his name as *Charles George* of New York City.[7]

MONDAY

Early on Monday Grace said "Goodby" to the Crumbs and climbed on board the "stage" for the eleven mile trip to DeRuyter. In the nineteenth century a railroad had been built along part of the route but the cost of building and maintaining its complex trestles was never met by the modest local traffic and the line was abandoned. Now the Otselic Valley was isolated again and Grace

The "Stage" that made the trip between South Otselic and DeRuyter.

rode into DeRuyter on a slow and uncomfortable wagon.

Grace knew just what to do when she arrived. She walked straight to the Tabor House and by 9:30 she was chatting in the kitchen with Mrs. Coye, the owner's wife. Mrs. Coye had known Grace for many years and the two talked for some time. In spite of her plans to parry questions from relatives, Grace made no effort to conceal her presence in the town.[8] Chester, after spending the night as Charles George, took his wake-up call and ate breakfast. Just what he was doing when Grace appeared two hours later is unknown, but by ten he and Grace were both in the sitting room talking earnestly. The northbound train was due to leave in forty minutes.

The two left the Tabor house separately and walked to the station. Several people who did not know Chester noticed the young man with the suitcase, tennis racket and umbrella. One young boy did know Chester. It was Harold Williams who lived on East Main Street in Cortland. Chester had boarded at the Williams house and knew Harold well. He told the boy he was going to Canastota and walked on to the station.[9]

At the Lehigh Valley station each bought a ticket to Canastota. When the 10:37 arrived Grace found a coach seat and sat by herself. Chester waited until the train started and then swung onto the platform of the last coach. He moved through the cars until he spotted Josephine Patrick and Gladys Westcott, girls whom Chester had known in Cortland.*

Chester chatted at length with the two young women. He told them that he was meeting a young man who was going to the Adirondacks where his uncle had a camp (cottage). Chester would be his guest. The girls were headed for the Adirondacks too and were to stay at Seventh Lake in the Fulton Chain. Chester expected to be 12 miles farther up the chain at Raquette Lake with his friend— or so he said—but would come down to Seventh Lake and call on the girls Thursday or Friday. He made no mention of Grace nor did he attempt to find her on the train.[10]

At Canastota a number of passengers left the train in order to transfer to an east-west line of the New York Central. Chester and Grace were among them. Chester approached the ticket agent and bought a New York Central mileage book, using the money his uncle had loaned him.[11]

---

*Chester didn't realize it but they were lucky to leave on time. That afternoon a cloudburst between Cortland and DeRuyter washed out the tracks and delayed later trains.

It had been a gray day with intermittent rain and during the afternoon they dropped the pretense of traveling apart and sat together. If Chester had any lingering plans of going to the Thousand Islands, they evaporated on the Canastota platform. He decided that it would be the Adirondacks. It was a critical decision, although there is no evidence that his conversation with Josephine Patrick and Gladys Westcott had played any part in it.

First it was necessary to go to Utica where Adirondack trains originated. It was afternoon and a poor time to start north. Darkness would soon come, obscuring the beautiful scenery and making it difficult to seek accommodations at the resort stations. The couple boarded an eastbound train for the thirty two mile trip to Utica, intending to spend the night there.

Utica was a large city by the standards of South Otselic but it was old stuff to Chester. He had "been around." Toward suppertime he took Grace to the Hotel Martin, a large modern house with a proper desk and bellboys. It was a giant step from the inn in DeRuyter where Chester had spent the previous night. It is unlikely that Billy had ever seen such a large building, much less slept in one. Chester went to the desk and registered, taking the key to room thirty-two.[12]

If Grace had nursed hopes of a surprise wedding at the end of the first day she was disappointed. Chester offered her no more than an evening of sightseeing up and down the main streets of Utica and the prospect of staying all night in a hotel. They ate in the hotel grill room and bought picture post cards of Utica and the nearby area.[13] Chester had established their identity when he registered. They were *Charles Gordon & Wife*, of New York City. At least Chester was consistent. He used the same initials every time.[14]

TUESDAY

Tuesday dawned as another warm July day with broken skies and the threat of frequent showers. Before leaving Utica Chester found time for a personal errand. He had been on the road for only two days yet he may have felt that his clothing would not last the trip. He took some clothes, including two shirts, to Leahy's Laundry on John Street. The clerk accepted the laundry and promised to forward it. The package would be sent by express to Old Forge, where it could be picked up by *Chester Gillette*.[15]

Then Chester and Grace made ready to travel. They took their bags to the rail station but on the way Chester "forgot" to pay his bill. No doubt the blame would be laid at the feet of Mr. Charles Gordon of New York!

80

The large, ornate rail station throbbed with activity and the big departure board listed some of the most famous trains in America, for the New York to Chicago trains of the New York Central all paused in Utica.

From the more distant platforms northern trains loaded and the young couple climbed on board the coaches that would take the route to Remsen, Fulton Chain and the Adirondacks. For Grace it was a journey into the unknown and she must have felt the excitement that wavers between anticipation and apprehension as she watched Utica slip behind.

The first hour of the trip was spent in climbing up out of the Mohawk Valley and into the foothills. Then the Adirondack journey really began. These were not alpine mountains and this was no trip through Switzerland. Most of the time the mountains were obscured by the dense forest that grew along the route. Still, it was a charming ride.

There were no real highways in the Adirondacks and the railroad was truly king. At the tiny stations gravel roads bordered the tracks and horse-drawn buggies arrived to meet each train. Tourists were driven to nearby lakes where they checked into huge wooden hotels, splendidly isolated on the shores of glittering water.

It wasn't really true, but passengers liked to believe that there wasn't a straight mile of track on the line. Indeed, the route seemed to twist and turn past endless lakes, cliffs, streams and deadwood swamps with only occasional glimpses of a distant peak. None of the mountains rises above 5,400 feet and most of them are forested on all but the steepest and highest slopes. If the last car had an observation platform it was popular summer sport to dodge the twisting smoke from the engine and attempt to spot deer standing next to dark pools of water.

Passengers on the Adirondack run were divided between tourists (who had no other way of entering the mountains) and the ambitious salesman trying to ply his trade in some isolated spot like Saranac Lake or Lake Clear Junction. Tourists clung to the windows but most salesmen had been here before. They slept or worked their way through the Utica newspapers. The hot story at the moment was the ongoing murder investigation involving Harry Thaw in New York City.[16]

Chester and Grace watched the little platform drama repeat itself at Fulton Chain, Big Moose, Beaver River and Sabattis. For some reason Chester had decided that they would go all the way to

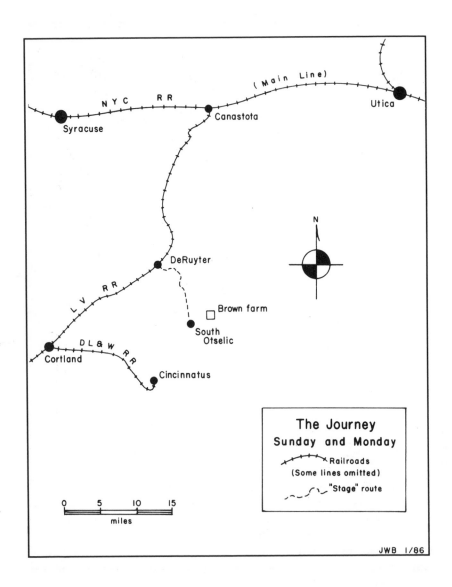

The Journey
Sunday and Monday

Railroads
(Some lines omitted)

"Stage" route

0 5 10 15
miles

JWB 1/86

82

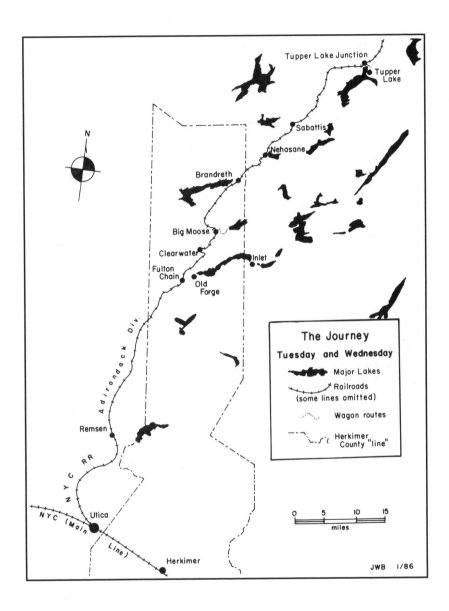

The Journey

Tuesday and Wednesday

Major Lakes

Railroads
(some lines omitted)

Wagon routes

Herkimer
County "line"

0   5   10   15
miles

N

Tupper Lake Junction
Tupper Lake

Sabattis

Nehasane

Brandreth

Big Moose

Clearwater

Inlet

Fulton
Chain

Old
Forge

Adirondack Div.

Remsen

N Y C R R

NYC (Main Line)

Utica

Herkimer

JWB 1/86

Tupper Lake, beyond the usual tourist sites. Here the railroad passed through an area of extensively cut over forest land. Toward late afternoon they drew into the station. If Chester had expected Tupper to be a repeat of the little platforms in the forest he was mistaken.

Tupper Lake was a big village bursting at the seams with sawmills and French Canadian lumbermen. The forest had been cut away for several miles and the lake could be seen in the distance. It was a large lake with booms of logs floating on the surface. This was no quiet tourist town.

What was worse, the railroad didn't really stop at Tupper Lake Village, but at Tupper Lake Junction, or Faust, two miles away. It was a long jolting ride in a wagon or "bus," before Chester and Grace found themselves on Park Street standing in front of a hotel—or what passed for one—the Alta Cliff Cottage. Because its owner was one Myron Newman it was sometimes called the Hotel Newman.

Chester asked the landlord for a room. Myron Newman was reluctant, and perhaps suspicious, but Chester claimed that he had written ahead for accommodations. Newman finally agreed to take the couple in for the night since it had been raining off and on that evening. However, the arrangement was to be for one night only.[17]

Chester signed in as *Charles George & Wife, N.Y.* The register showed that several families in the hotel were from New York City as was Myron Newman, himself.[18] Chester may have had second thoughts about posing as a city resident but if he did it was then too late. He continued to talk with Newman.

When the couple ate at the Alta Cliff that night the waitress noted that Grace was highly agitated. Later she claimed that the girl was near hysteria and that Chester spoke roughly to her.[19] After supper Chester and Grace went for a walk down Park Street toward the center of the village. On returning Chester again engaged Newman in conversation, asking about places that would have more lakes or mountain scenery. Newman made several suggestions and Chester talked of going back down toward Raquette Lake.[20]

WEDNESDAY

The relationship between Chester and Grace was reaching a crisis and it failed to improve during the night. At breakfast in the Alta Cliff dining room they were served by Clara Greenwood, the same waitress they had seen the night before. Again Grace seemed

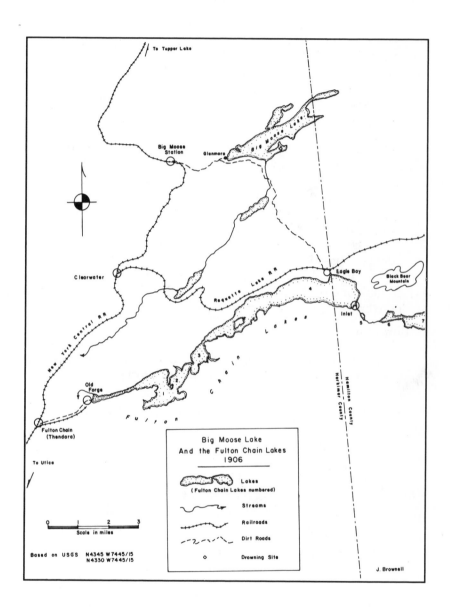

To Tupper Lake

Big Moose
Station

Glenmore

Big Moose Lake

Clearwater

Raquette Lake RR

Eagle Bay

Black Bear
Mountain

4

Inlet

5   6   7

New York Central RR

3

Chain   Lakes

Old
Forge

Fulton

Hamilton County
Herkimer County

Fulton Chain
(Thendara)

To Utica

Big Moose Lake
And the Fulton Chain Lakes
1906

Lakes
(Fulton Chain Lakes numbered)

Streams

Railroads

Dirt Roads

○   Drowning Site

0   1   2   3
Scale in miles

Based on USGS   N4345 W7445/15
                N4330 W7445/15

J. Brownell

85

upset and when Chester rose and left the room Grace went to Clara, threw her arms round her and burst into tears.[21]

There was little chance in Tupper Lake of slipping away without paying the bill. Indeed Newman, himself, called for a bus to take the couple to the station. Once outside they waited on the sidewalk. Across the street young eleven-year old Ed Timmons and his mother watched Grace follow behind Chester crying bitterly. Things were not going well at all.[22]

At Tupper Lake Junction the couple waited for the morning "down" train at 6:45 a.m. Chester had his mileage book so tickets were not required. However, they checked Grace's trunk through to Old Forge before boarding the coach. The ride back through the mountains was a repetition of the previous day's trip, although there were only about a dozen people in the car. Those who gossiped about the Thaw murder case had a new morsel to digest. Harry Thaw was facing a charge of murder and his attorneys were talking of a defense based on insanity.

But Grace and Chester had other things to do and talk about. Grace took one of the post cards Chester had bought in Utica and wrote a brief message to her mother:

Dear Mother:
    Am having a lovely time. Don't worry. Will write you more to-night about the trip. It was rather unexpected but am glad we are here. Love to all the girls & have them in school. Lovingly,

                               Billy[23]

If Grace was worried or distraught she tried not to betray it to her mother. On the other hand she spoke confidently of "the trip" as if her family would understand immediately her sudden vacation in the Adirondacks.

Chester, too, took time to write a post card, but this was business. The previous week his cousin and next door neighbor, Ella Hoag, had pointed out that he could not draw ahead on his salary. Now he tried again, sending a post card to her at the factory:

    Please send five dollars ($5) to Eagle Bay, N.Y. so that I can get it Friday.

                               Chester[24]

Eagle Bay was not on the main railroad line but was a village on the long series of lakes called the Fulton Chain. Old Forge lay on First Lake, at one end of the chain. Eagle Bay, on Fourth Lake, was reasonably close to Big Moose Lake. Chester would have to stay in the Adirondacks to collect the money should his cousin honor his request.

One of the two decided that they should leave the train and see more of the lakes. (Hardly a railroad station on the line was situated directly on a lakeshore.) But Grace's trunk was on its way to Old Forge. Any stopover would be a brief one. They both left the train at Big Moose and sought transportation to Big Moose Lake slightly over a mile away.

The "bus" was driven by James McAllister and during the ride to the lake Grace plied him with questions about later trains that would go on toward Old Forge. In the end she decided that they would take the late train that night. It was a curious choice, for they would not reach Fulton Chain Station until after midnight and Old Forge was a two-mile ride from that station.[25]

McAllister also took the two post cards which Chester had forgotten to post on the train. He promptly mailed them on his next trip to the station. One card arrived at Cortland that night and the other in South Otselic next day. It was an age in which railroads really delivered the mail![26]

McAllister drove Chester and Grace directly to the Glennmore Hotel. The Glennmore typified the nineteenth century Adirondack resort hotel. It was big, built of wood, and dominated by its porches.

Hotel Glennmore, Big Moose, circa 1907.

Between the basement and the attic were three floors of public rooms and guest rooms. It was surrounded by trees and outbuildings but only fifty yards down the slope was the shore of Big Moose Lake. From the porch one could look eastward across the water to Covey's point a mile away. Beyond that the lake divided into bays and the eastern most areas were hidden from the hotel.

The manager at the desk was Andrew Morrison. Chester indicated that they were not interested in staying the night but would like to take the steamboat ride around the lake, eat dinner at the hotel, and return to the late train.

Morrison thought that this was a bit too much, for the steamboat ride was a long one and they might miss dinner. He suggested that Chester rent a boat from the boat livery operated by his father down at the lake shore. The couple could be back in plenty of time for dinner and easily make the southbound train. Chester agreed and signed the hotel register.[27]

But this time Chester did something very unusual. He no longer claimed to be married to the girl who traveled with him. Perhaps this was because they were not going to stay the night. In any event he

The Boathouse at the Hotel Glennmore. The little steamboat is just visible to the left. On the shore is the fatal rowboat, crated and ready for shipment to the county seat as evidence for the trial.

Big Moose Lake from the Glennmore dock looking east. South Bay, where Grace drowned, lies behind the south shore trees on the right.

filled in a separate line on the register for each of them. On the top line he wrote *Carl Grahm, Albany.* Beneath this he wrote *Grace Brown, S. Otselic.*[28]

Chester gathered up his suitcase along with the tennis racket and umbrella. Grace hung her hat in the lobby and followed Chester down the slope to the boathouse. It was late in the morning and Morrison's concern about timing was directed at the lateness of the steamboat departure rather than the length of the trip.

Chester and Grace had the entire afternoon before them as they rented a boat. The elder Morrison (father of the desk clerk) offered Chester a rowboat which had just been cleaned out. Grace sat in the stern as Chester pushed away and started rowing across the lake, staying close to the south shore. Morrison stood wondering why the young man had taken along a suitcase, a tennis racket and an umbrella.[29]

It was a good day, and for a change, one without rain. The couple were seen rowing along the southern side of the lake and past Covey's Camp. Cottagers along the south side of South Bay watched the man and girl that afternoon as they rowed back and forth and even stopped on the shore, apparently for a picnic.

By dinnertime the boat had not returned. It was not unusual. Vacationers tended to forget themselves on the lake and boaters would often stop at other camps along the shore to take a meal. The long summer evenings stretched out the hours that the public spent on the lake. When the sun finally sank behind the mountain and the boat was still missing Morrison was not immediately worried. If the couple was trapped by darkness they would, no doubt, spend the night at someone's cottage along the shore. The hotel would wait until daylight.

THURSDAY

By morning there was still no word of the missing boat. Now it was time to worry. The steamboat lit off its boiler and was soon under way. It commenced to circle the lake blowing its whistle—cottagers along the lake knew what that meant. Someone was presumed to be lost in the woods. The steamboat whistle would give them a bearing back to the lake. The story quickly spread among the camp owners that a boat was missing from the Glennmore. A large scale search would be organized, first on the lake, and then in the woods.

Jean Brown, a twelve year old girl whose family owned a camp on the north shore was caught up in the excitement of the search. She rowed to Covey's near the middle of the lake and found that adults everywhere were beginning to take part.

She was asked to row to a camp on the south shore and request the use of a boat. On her way across South Bay she encountered the still, ominous sight of an overturned boat floating on the surface. There was no sign of life anywhere on the bay. She quickly pulled back to Covey's to tell the news.[30]

The steamboat was hailed and dispatched to South Bay. Here its small crew secured the boat and began to search the water. The thirteen year old purser of the tiny forty foot steamer was Roy Higby. Peering over the side Higby spotted a white blob in the dark waters of the bay. Men in rowboats grappled for the sunken form and hauled on board the steamer the body of a dead girl. It was Grace Brown.[31]

The crew searched for the rest of the day but found only a man's hat and a woman's coat. There was no sign of Carl Grahm, his suitcase, his tennis racket or his umbrella. He had vanished into thin air.

Death Certificate for Grace Brown. Note that the cause of death was amended in December to include the autopsy conclusion.

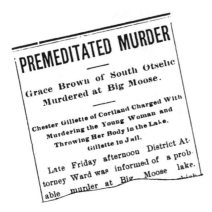

9

INTO THE
PUBLIC EYE

Carl Grahm *had* disappeared, but Chester Gillette was very much alive. On the evening of that fateful Wednesday Chester scrambled ashore on the south side of Big Moose Lake. He was cold and soaking wet. Behind him in the lake was the dim shape of the overturned boat but there was neither sight nor sound of Billy Brown.

For the twenty-two year old man it was a staggering, even overwhelming, moment. Yet Chester did not look for the nearest cottage. He did not walk along the shore to find help. He made no attempt to return to the hotel.

Instead, Chester carefully made his way through the woods to the spot where the couple had recently picnicked. By accident, or possibly by design, Chester had left his suitcase there. He now changed into dry clothes and gathering up his suitcase, tennis racket and camera, he headed south through the forest.[1]

He quickly came to the road that winds its way to Eagle Bay on Fourth Lake. Evening was now coming and as he passed the bridge over the outlet he encountered three men who were walking north toward Big Moose. They exchanged greetings, but Chester pushed on.[2] Those four miles along the woods road took him from the Big Moose camping community to the Fulton Chain. This string of beautiful lakes had its own community of summer people, hotels and local transportation. (See map on page 85.)

Once on the Fulton Chain Chester could go up and down the lakes by steamboat from Old Forge on First Lake to Inlet on the

Fourth.* It seemed like a different world, and Chester probably hoped that it was. He strode into Eagle Bay with his baggage and camera but the tennis racket, like Carl Grahm, had disappeared.

Darkness had fallen when Chester stopped to look over Eagle Bay. For some reason he preferred to move on to the south shore of Fourth Lake. Perhaps Eagle Bay was physically and emotionally linked to Big Moose. At any rate, Chester walked down to the village dock and when the steamboat arrived at 9:30 Chester boarded. It was the last eastbound trip of the day for the little *Uncas* and Chester rode across the lake to the village of Inlet.³

At Inlet he made his way to the Arrowhead Hotel, another rambling, long-porched Adirondack institution. Chester strode up to the desk with suitcase and camera. He chatted casually with the proprietor and asked about room rates. There was no question now about his identity. He wrote down *Chester Gillette, Cortland* and took his baggage to room 24. He was the last guest to register at the Arrowhead that day.⁴ Grace Brown had been dead less than six hours.

By Thursday morning Chester had settled into the vacation that he had discussed with his friends in Cortland, his uncle, and more recently with Josephine Patrick and Gladys Westcott. He had told the latter that he would spend the early part of the week at Raquette Lake and then might come down to the Fulton Chain. Now Chester *was* at Fourth Lake and he began to make plans to head east toward Seventh Lake where the two Cortland girls were staying.

First, however, Chester had to pull together some loose ends. He needed money and only the day before he had mailed a postcard to Ella Hoag asking for five dollars. But she was to send the money to Eagle Bay and Chester had chosen to stay at Inlet. He went to the Inlet Post office and pointed out that he might have mail over at Eagle Bay. The obliging postmaster gave him a postcard and suggested that he send the Eagle Bay postmaster a simple instruction to forward his mail to the Arrowhead at Inlet. Chester promptly mailed the card.⁵

He next looked for ways of getting to Seventh Lake. Inlet was, as the name implies, located at the point where the major stream entered Fourth Lake. Farther up the stream were Fifth, Sixth and Seventh Lakes. He asked about renting a canoe and was directed to

---

*The first four lakes differ only slightly in surface elevation, and some are merely arms of others. There was, in 1906, a regular steamboat service which touched at villages and major hotels.

the landing. Chester was adept at paddling canoes—he had done this often at Cortland. Now he headed toward the upper lakes.

It wasn't as easy as paddling on a lake. The current was against him and for part of the way it was necessary to carry the canoe, but Chester made it all the way to Seventh Lake. Toward evening he stopped at Seventh Lake House, a hotel on the shore of Seventh Lake . He signed the register and made no attempt to conceal his identity. He was *Chester Gillette* of Cortland.[6]

He ordered a supper and conversed freely with the innkeeper. When asked about Black Bear Mountain and the trails that led to the top, the proprietor took Chester outside and pointed out the mountain across the lake. Chester paddled back to Fourth Lake without seeing the two girls from Cortland. It was getting dark.[7]

That evening Chester talked at length with the Reverend Mr. Dean who was also staying at the Arrowhead with his family. Chester was still interested in Black Bear Mountain and so were the Deans. A climb was set for the next day.[8]

On Friday morning Chester made ready for the day's trip. However, there was another loose end to tidy up. He had appeared at the Arrowhead on Wednesday night with dry clothing, but in his suitcase he carried damp underclothes and trousers. These he hung on hooks in his room but the heavy trousers were painfully slow to dry. On Friday morning Chester took the pants to the innkeeper and asked if they could be cleaned and pressed. Valet service was not usually offered at Adirondack hotels but the innkeeper promised to do his best.[9]

Chester then went off to climb the mountain. Climbing is, perhaps, the wrong word, for even the highest of Adirondack peaks can be reached on walking trails and Black Bear is a small mountain indeed. Its peak is less than 1,000 feet above the waters of Fourth Lake. However, visitors considered it obligatory to climb the mountain at least once and Chester went off in the company of the Deans. Chester was in fine form and Gertrude Dean, the daughter, was most impressed. Everyone enjoyed the trip.[10]

Josephine Patrick and Gladys Westcott climbed Black Bear Mountain that day too, but Chester didn't meet them on the trails. He did encounter the girls in one of the Inlet stores afterward. Two whole days had passed since the boat ride on Big Moose Lake. Chester was charming, the girls were agreeable and life was becoming increasingly pleasant.

There was one remaining task for Chester. The laundry in Utica had been instructed to ship his clothing to Old Forge, yet Chester was staying on Fourth Lake. He had already arranged to have his mail forwarded. Now he took steps to get his laundry. He boarded the steamship at the landing that Friday night and sought help from Captain Hoffman who was about to steam back to Old Forge for the night.[11]

Hoffman was more than willing to help the young man but he didn't want to claim the wrong package. He took out a company envelope and asked Chester to write his name on the back just to be sure. Chester promptly wrote *Chester Gillette.* Hoffman cast off and returned to Old Forge. If the laundry was there Hoffman could pick it up before the first run on Saturday.[12]

Friday night was one of those mellow occasions that prompt people to talk later about the "Good old days." The hotel guests sang on the porches and in the lobby. They played games and watched the waning moon shimmer on the rippling lake. Chester chatted with several of the young ladies who stayed at the hotel. He was now firmly established at the Arrowhead. It was Friday the thirteenth but things couldn't have been better. Chester went to his room to sleep.

Had Chester known what was happening elsewhere he might have found it difficult to sleep. After the steamboat had brought the body of the dead girl back to the Glennmore dock on Thursday, the hotel notified the county seat and asked for help. The web that Chester was braiding in one part of the Adirondacks was beginning to unravel in another.

Coroner Isaac Coffin arrived on the scene next day and inspected the body. He noted bruises to the head and listened to the searchers' accounts of their unsuccessful attempts to find the elusive Carl Grahm. By Friday afternoon he reported his findings to the county seat. Herkimer, like Cortland, had for a county seat a community bearing the same name as the county.

Regional newspapers were already carrying accounts of the death and the presence of the coroner. Coffin had come to a tentative conclusion of "foul play" and news reporters immediately snatched this phrase for inclusion in their copy. Back in Cortland the *Standard* gave the story two columns on an inside page, noting that the victim had been working in the city. The case of the missing Grahm was dangled as bait and the reader was led to believe that more was to follow.[13]

More *did* follow, and quickly. By dinnertime Coroner Coffin's report had reached the district attorney. George W. Ward was a lawyer of considerable courtroom skill and a healthy political ambition. It may have been the latter which prompted him to grasp at Coffin's suspicion that there was foul play at Big Moose. District Attorney Ward was running for office in November. After having served as public prosecutor he now sought the post of county judge.

He quickly came to the conclusion that the coroner was right. The disappearance of Grahm made the drowning look more and more suspicious. Ward decided that this case was to be handled properly—and personally. He called the county sheriff and secured the services of deputy sheriff Granville Ingraham and undersheriff Austin Klock. These men prepared to accompany Ward on an investigation of the death site.[14]

The two officers met Ward at the county seat on Friday evening and set out for Big Moose. In any other New York State county travel would have been a simple thing in 1906, but Herkimer County was different. On the map it presents a long vertical rectangle with the populated southern end in the Mohawk Valley and its northern towns in the Adirondacks. There was no direct rail communication between the south where the county seat was located, and the lake country where Grace Brown had died.

First it was necessary to leave Herkimer and travel west to Utica. Then one had to wait for the less frequent trains that took the northern route through the mountains. Getting to Utica was easy— the east-west tracks of the New York Central represented one of the busiest rail routes in America. But the next train north was the Adirondack Limited at 1:25 a.m. Ward arranged with the railroad for special stops to be made for him on the express northward but there was to be a long wait in the cavernous Utica station before departing.[15]

At this point Ward enjoyed a stroke of very good fortune. Although the waiting room was not crowded at the midnight hour, talk about the tragic drowning was brisk. Ward was known to a number of people in the station but it was a stranger who approached the men from Herkimer and asked about their trip to Big Moose. Ward and the two officers were inclined to put off such questions but the young man surprised them by volunteering the fact that he had known the victim![16]

The newcomer identified himself as Bert Gross and accompanied the trio on the northbound train. He readily explained that he had known Grace Brown at the factory in Cortland where he was a superintendent. Bert Gross rambled at length and provided an extremely helpful picture of young Billy Brown. For example she

97

had been keeping company with another young man in the Gillette Factory. The young man was, in fact, a friend of Gross—a friend named Chester Gillette.

The investigators sat and listened with growing interest. All three noted that Chester's initials were also those of the missing Carl Grahm. What did Chester Gillette look like? Bert Gross could give a fairly accurate description. It was familiar.

Would Gross know where Chester was at the moment? By coincidence he did. Chester was taking a vacation in the Adirondacks. Only Wednesday he had sent to his cousin in Cortland a request for money. Gross had that very post card right in his pocket and he showed the astounded officials the message that Chester had written on the train less that three days earlier.[17]

The little group of officers snapped up the post card and Ward took young Gross under his wing. The Herkimer men had intended to disembark at Big Moose but now their attention was drawn to Eagle Bay on Fourth Lake—part of the Fulton Chain Lakes. As they rattled northward on the train Ward changed plans. The death site could wait. The entire party paused at Fulton Chain station, just two miles from Old Forge.

The little delegation reached Fulton Chain at 3:25 a.m. The temptation to go on to Big Moose had been great. The temptation to forge ahead to Eagle Bay where Chester was expecting to find money was even greater. But Ward was now receiving tips that luggage and parcels relating to the dead or missing people might be found on trains or in baggage rooms. Moreover, he hated to leave Fulton Chain station uncovered. If his quarry were in the Fulton Chain area all escape routes to the south would funnel through that little rail station.

By daybreak they discovered that the laundry package from Utica had arrived in the Adirondacks and had been sent on to Old Forge. Now Ward decided to split his forces. He sent deputy Ingraham into Old Forge to watch for the package. Ingraham did not wait for a train on the short line but took the "stage" to Old Forge. The laundry package was there, waiting to be claimed. After telling the baggage agent to watch the package a very hungry and tired Ingraham went off to find breakfast.[18]

He barely made it. At 7:00 a.m. Captain Hoffman appeared at the baggage office with Chester Gillette's name and oral instruction to collect the package. A messenger brought deputy Ingraham on the run and Ingraham took the steamboat himself. The red hot trail now pointed to the Arrowhead Hotel on Fourth Lake.[19]

But Ward knew nothing of this. He had already started off on the other trail, taking Gross and undersheriff Klock with him. He could have reached Eagle Bay by steamboat later in the day but there was an alternative.

Ward went on to Clearwater Station, half way to Big Moose. Here another private line left the New York Central and wound eastward through the Adirondacks, The Raquette Lake Railroad, brainchild of William West Durant, who owned property in the area, also touched at Eagle Bay. Ward was on his way. There was only one train—one that left Clearwater when the afternoon train from New York arrived. If Ward used the railroad as his deputies later claimed, he did it with commandeered equipment.

It was still early in the day when Ward, Klock and an excited young Gross stepped down at Eagle Bay. The three went straight to the hotel and inspected the register. There was no Chester Gillette, nor had any young man of his description checked in that week. Ward was stymied, but only for a moment. On impulse he strode to the post office and asked if there was mail for Chester Gillette.[20]

The postmaster seemed unconcerned about privacy of the mails. He volunteered that there was no mail for Chester. But only the day before he had received a postal card *from* Chester Gillette asking that mail be forwarded across the lake to the Arrowhead Hotel!

The Arrowhead Hotel at Inlet where Chester was arrested.

Suddenly the trail was hot again. Ward scooped up the post card as evidence and the three raced to the dock where they took over a steamboat that was making a stop at Eagle Bay. They quickly crossed to Inlet and the Arrowhead Hotel. Deputy Ingraham, who was closing in on the same target, was still on the lakes, slowly making his way east on the mail boat.

Quite unaware of what was happening, Chester ate a leisurely breakfast in the Arrowhead's dining room. When he finished he stepped into the lobby only to see the familiar face of Bert Gross whom he greeted with a friendly wave. Bert blurted out the news:

"Chester, don't you know that Billy Brown is drowned?"

"No!" Chester answered, "Is that so?"

Gross had almost played out his role in the little drama for the men next asked Chester if he could account for his actions between Monday and Wednesday. The question was heavy with implication.

"No," Chester replied, "I don't know as I can."[21] With that answer Chester's fortunes began to crumble. He was placed under arrest.

In that simple age, over a half century ago, Chester's arrest and questioning were informal in the extreme. They did warn Chester that anything he said might be held against him but Chester's first concern was paying for his room. He had no money, for he still hadn't heard from Ella Hoag. He asked the men from Herkimer to pay his account for him. Neither Chester nor his captors thought much further about the rights of the accused.[22]

Ward had arrested Chester in Hamilton County and now it was necessary to arraign him in the county where the crime had taken place. All four boarded the little steamboat and cast off for the Herkimer County village of Old Forge. As the steamboat entered Third Lake it passed the mailboat on its way "up." The officials recognized deputy Ingraham standing on the deck of the eastbound boat. They ordered both steamboats to stop and hauled Ingraham and his package of laundry on board.[23]

The officials set up an impromptu command post at the Old Forge House. Crowds of townspeople and guests watched the law officers march Chester into the hotel. They placed Chester in a room and took turns guarding him while Ward sent for a justice of the peace, James H. Higby. (It had been Higby's son who had seen the body from the steamboat on Thursday morning). By noon the justice had arrived and held a preliminary examination. He ordered that

Chester be held for the grand Jury. It was a very brief arraignment.[24]

In the meantime Ward used the telephone to make contact with those who had encountered Chester earlier in the week. The owner of the Arrowhead and many of his guests had already identified Chester. Now it was the turn of those who worked at Big Moose. By train, boat and road they came to Old Forge and pointed to the man they had known as Carl Grahm.[25]

During the day Grace's trunk was located and opened. In it were letters Chester had written. Chester did not deny this when questioned. He did not deny taking Grace to Big Moose Lake, but his story of the row on that lake was one of accident and panic and a girl who could not swim.

By afternoon all preliminary questioning was over. Ward had obtained the confirmation he needed to support his original suspicion. Gillette *was* Carl Grahm. He *had* been with Grace when she died. And he *had* left the death scene stealthily after the tragedy. They handcuffed Chester and boarded the southbound train.

Afternoon newspapers had announced the arrest of the Cortland man and his transfer to the county seat. Crowds of people pressed close to the train at every stop and strangers boarded the car and pushed down the aisle for a glimpse of the captive. At Utica, where the party changed to the main line train, the curious craned their necks to see the alleged murderer.[26]

It was nearly sundown when the train arrived in Herkimer. A crowd of nearly two thousand had gathered for a glimpse of the prisoner. In less than a week Chester had cascaded from obscurity to the center of public attention.

10

TRIAL BY PRESS

CROWDS SEE GILLETTE

Visitors Pass by the Cell Door in Single File

AT PRISONER'S INVITATION

Was Exasperated by Number of Witnesses to Identify Him—Wanted to Do It All At Once—Not Willing to Talk .on Subject of Murder, But Ready For Other Topics.

Herkimer, July 26.—

Chester was immediately remanded to the Herkimer county jail where he was confined to a cell on an upper floor. It was an ancient jail and poorly lighted. The entire front of the room was a grille of steel bars while the floor, ceiling and interior walls were of stone and steel plates. It was thoroughly depressing.

Chester awoke to find that his first full day in jail was a Sunday. He attended the services that were provided for prisoners and readily participated. He even sang. Otherwise he quickly found that confinement was oppressive. He paced the cell and often sat with his head in his hands. At times he was allowed to walk around the corridor and talk with prisoners in other cells.[1]

The local newspapers, which had so diligently followed the drowning and search were, for the most part, weekday papers and did not publish on Sunday, yet the ripple was widening. Even as Chester spent his first Sunday in jail the austere *New York Times,* 200 miles away, carried an accurate account of the death and arrest on an inside page.[2]

Curiosity about Chester mounted, but the authorities decided to keep the prisoner from the public. He was to be allowed no visitors except for family and attorneys. Local reporters besieged the jailkeepers for information. Other regional papers made ready to copy the Utica and Herkimer stories and many prepared to send writers directly to Herkimer. A good story by "our own reporter" would be just the thing.

Monday was the start of a busy week—the first of many.

Chester had no choice. He could only adapt to the routine of the jail, but reporters smelled a sensational story. The prosecutor had already implied that this was no ordinary murder—no illiterate immigrant striking a fellow worker with a shovel—this was a case involving a middle class American. The widely reported story of Harry Thaw in New York City did not help. The press had discovered that the public possesses an insatiable appetite for crime involving "good" families.

Central New York newspapers clamored for stories about Chester. They began to search his background and found that it was far more varied than that of the young farm girl who had died. Chester made good copy. Who else had been born in the Montana territory? Who else had been to Hawaii? Who in Herkimer County had gone to Oberlin College?

Reporters pressed the jail officials for details of the young man's confinement. Before the week was out they were listing what he was eating, what he was drinking; what he read, and (when they could get the information), who sent letters to him. The New York Times was a day behind in treating the story of the death on the lake and the subsequent capture. Papers both upstate and down played up the inconsistencies in Chester's various stories about the accident.[3]

In the first full week after the tragedy District Attorney Ward set out to prepare his case. He sent investigators to Big Moose to interview employees and guests of the hotel. One clue led to another. Various people had passed Chester on his way to Eagle Bay and in short order the officers had traced his footsteps from Big Moose Lake to the Arrowhead Hotel, to Seventh Lake and Black Bear Mountain.

One representative went to Cortland. Accompanied by police chief Erving E. Barnes, Charles Dowd went to East Main Street where Chester had roomed. In the upstairs room that had been Chester's was a desk and in it they found letters—all the letters that Billy had frantically written from South Otselic.[4] In their enthusiasm they missed one letter which had been left elsewhere in the room. Lizzie Crain, the landlady, found it three weeks later.[5]

There were a few missing pieces. When Chester left the Glennmore with the rowboat he had with him both an umbrella and a tennis racket. He brought neither into Inlet the night that he walked out of the woods. Suspecting that one or the other might have been a murder weapon, Ward pressed hard for their recovery. But there was nothing missing about the rowboat. It was crated and shipped off to the county seat. It promised to be the largest exhibit of the forthcoming trial.

Working back from the Glennmore Hotel the officers found James McAllister who had driven the couple from the rail station to the hotel and who had mailed their postcards for them. McAllister pointed out that the couple had arrived on the southbound train, coming from Tupper Lake. Ward's men put the driver on their list of potential witnesses and proceeded north to Tupper.

In short order the team of officers found Chester's entries in the hotel registers at Tupper Lake, Utica and DeRuyter. Chester's carefully contrived pseudonyms quickly fell apart. In every case the hotel clerks turned in perfect descriptions of the traveller. In DeRuyter there were witnesses who had known both Chester and Grace. Even passengers on the train were tracked down. A noose was slowly drawing around Chester even as he sat in the Herkimer jail.

In less than a week Ward had collected an impressive mass of evidence and was readying it for the courtroom. He was uncommonly generous with the men and women of the press and newspapers immediately printed every detail of Chester's vacation itinerary. Central New York residents and vacationers alike combed the papers looking for the names of familiar people and places.

In case the reader should miss the point to which all this evidence led, Ward gave the press a personal viewpoint: "This fellow is a degenerate, and all circumstances point to the belief that he knocked the girl senseless and threw her overboard."[6]

Not to be outdone, Coroner Coffin added his personal conclusion: "There is scarcely any doubt but that Miss Brown was taken out on the lake and deliberately murdered."[7] Both men were quoted faithfully throughout the state and many reporters rather expected Chester to "crack" and confess to the murder.

But Chester maintained that he was innocent. If anything he seemed to relish being the center of attention, grim as that position was. Reporters wrote to him. Friends wrote to him. A man in Indiana wrote claiming that Chester was a nephew.[8] Even total strangers wrote to Chester—particularly women. Yet Chester appeared not to be overly worried about obtaining legal counsel—and counsel he would need. Already Ward was planning to approach the governor and ask for a special term of Supreme Court just to try this one case.

In the face of the dark image he had acquired in the press Chester could expect little help from the outside. His family was far away and nearly penniless. His parents who, themselves, had worked with Salvation Army programs dealing with prisons, were only just discovering that their oldest son was in jail. Chester was slow to inform the family, and his mother received much of the early news from newspapers—not, perhaps, the most impartial of sources.

Ironically, the Gillettes had deserted the Dowie movement which, in turn, had lured them from the Salvation Army. They left Zion City bag and baggage, and were now scratching out a living in the small mining town of Fraser, Colorado.

Horace Gillette, the industrialist who had once adopted the trappings of protector and sponsor now vacillated. Many people in Cortland expected him to spring to Chester's aid, if only because he was "family." But now, in the face of notoriety, he suddenly became cautious. His public statements were brief and guarded. He seemed willing to help Chester, but only after looking more deeply into the horrible affair. Perhaps if Chester were to make a strong case of innocence.

But Horace did not travel to Herkimer. Rather, he sent a cousin, Fred Gillette a local jeweler and brother of Ella Hoag. Accompanied by a young attorney, Fred twice visited Chester in his jail cell. Next day they returned home presumably to report to Horace. Horace remained silent.[9]

Still, rumors persisted that Chester's defense would be arranged through Cortland lawyers and that the lawyers would be engaged by the family. But the family managed to remain circumspect. While they continued to assert that Chester was not to be deserted, they made no move at all to provide him with counsel in Herkimer.

Chester's friends in Cortland were neither monied nor influential. They were mostly the young men with whom Chester had hung out. They read in the newspapers that a strong circumstantial case was being mounted against their friend and noted the long delay in providing him with counsel. At last a few of Chester's chums sought out a Cortland lawyer and asked what might be done.[10]

Oddly, the lawyer they approached was Byron A. Benedict, a former district attorney who commuted to a healthy practice in Syracuse. It was his daughter whom Chester had taken to Raymond's on the Fourth. Benedict was probably unaware of that particular dinner date and would have been thoroughly shaken had he known that George Ward, in Herkimer was already weaving it into the case against Chester.

Benedict chose not to involve himself, but he did recommend a lawyer in Herkimer County who might prove useful. The Herkimer lawyer was a former state senator and district attorney, A. M. Mills.[11] The press had already linked Senator Mills with the mission Horace Gillette had sent to Herkimer, but again nothing was done and Mills was not retained. Chester was to sit and wait a while longer.

And Chester could ill afford to wait. The district attorney's case was strengthened daily with the accumulation of evidence in the county court house. Ward was confident that his request for a special term of court would be granted, and with it would come a grand jury which could issue an indictment against Chester. The district attorney needed but a fraction of his evidence to ensure that Chester would stand trial.

But Ward was deliberate and thorough in his preparation. These efforts were treated in detail in the local press and were already receiving more space than was normally used in reporting actual trials. Even as the search went on the district attorney's office continued to serve subpoenas throughout the Adirondacks.

Ward's zeal for gathering evidence drew criticism even as the search went on. Herkimer County had a small population and a very modest county budget, but Ward was threatening to expend tens of thousands of dollars gathering witnesses and evidence. In 1906 such sums were staggering to consider.

Chester had neither the opportunity nor the expertise to defend his own interests. A defense counsel, had there been one, would have been busy gathering his own evidence, interviewing witnesses and above all, watching the district attorney, for Ward continued to chip away at Chester's past.

Ward's intense preparations may have been more than coincidence. The November elections were a mere four months away. A friend might have commented that Ward was getting his groundwork done so that it would not become entangled with the political campaign later. An enemy would have been quick to suggest that the flood of publicity accompanying the investigation could scarcely harm his candidacy. Only the unkindest of enemies would claim that George Ward was actively seeking publicity.

Whether it was sought or not, publicity continued to place the little upstate village and county in the national limelight. It was not always flattering. After the early establishment of rules limiting access to the prisoner, the system appeared to fail. Rather than ask to visit Chester, crowds of strangers requested tours of the jail. This was hardly an everyday practice in normal times, but now great lines of visitors trooped through the maze of stairs and alleyways that comprised the county jail. The lines slowed near Chester's cell where the curious peeked through the bars for a look at the famous criminal whose name was in the newspapers daily.[12]

Chester's older sister, Hazel, was in New York State when she discovered her brother's predicament. She traveled straight to Herkimer where, as a relative, she was permitted to visit her brother. Those who were in a position to watch claimed that Chester showed emotion for the first time since he was arrested.[13]

By the end of July the authorities finally put a stop to the sightseeing in the county jail—or at least they attempted to limit it. Henceforth outsiders could visit the facility only on Mondays.[14] Those who followed Chester's progress in the press learned that he was now permitted a gas stove with which to heat his meals. He read avidly both books and magazines. Predictably, some thought that the gas burner was a frill and that his reading should be limited to religious literature.[15]

The recent limitation on visitors failed to curb the curious entirely. One of the public visitors to the jail was Carrie Gleason from Herkimer. Carrie was a mother with sons of her own and she was intensely curious about the young man who was being held. To her surprise Chester came to the bars and spoke pleasantly. She left with a very favorable impression of the young prisoner.[16]

On August first, George Ward went to the state capitol to request the special term of Supreme Court. The governor responded quickly. Within twenty-four hours an extraordinary term was set and Justice Irving R. Devendorf was appointed to preside. The special term would commence on August twenty seventh.[17]

Many lay people were misled by the August date and expected a full murder trial to take place. Actually the special term had some housekeeping to accomplish. First there would be a grand jury which would decide if Chester was to be held for trial. If it should indict the young man, the court still had to choose a panel of potential jurors prior to the start of an actual trial.

A grand jury was set for late in August, and the public was instructed that a jury trial, if Chester were indicted, would not be held until November. This would carefully place the trial after the fall elections and, presumably, take the Gillette case out of the realm of politics.

Interviewers continued to be impressed with Chester's coolness and speculated that he might not be aware of the seriousness of the situation. Ward continued to press. After numerous questionings, Chester volunteered some information about the missing tennis racket. A party of searchers under the direction of sheriff Richard found the racket, slightly the worse for wear, beneath a log not far from the road that Chester had walked from Big Moose to Eagle Bay.[18]

As the grand jury time approached, the press questioned whether Horace Gillette would stand by his nephew. Bert Gross appeared in Herkimer and talked again with Chester. He also sought out young Charles Thomas, a local lawyer.[19] Speculation now swayed between Senator Mills and Charles Thomas as the defense attorney, but no word came from Cortland about their retention. The *Cortland Standard* wrote a story: "Gillette Not Deserted," yet nothing in the story suggested help from the Gillette family.[20]

When Undersheriff Klock returned from Big Moose with the tennis racket he visited Chester in his cell. Would Chester like some water lilies that Klock had picked in the lake where Grace drowned? Chester did want them, but he drew fire from the local newspaper:

> It is safe to say that he does not need the flowers to remind him of the girl he so foully wronged, in fact the wonder is that he can look at them without suffering.[21]

On August ninth Chester turned twenty three. His birthday was celebrated in jail and duly reported in the press. But it was a party without family, friends or joy.[22]

The Herkimer County Jail

109

By the middle of August Undersheriff Klock was in Cortland serving subpoenas. There was considerable interest in knowing who was to be called to testify. At the head of the list were Ella Hoag, Horace Gillette and Harriet Benedict. It was a long list and included co-workers, landladies and the Cortland police chief, Erving Barnes.[23] As the grand jury date approached the pace of events quickened. Ella Hoag and her brother Fred Gillette conferred with Senator Mills. The press speculated that these emissaries were fronting for Horace Gillette of Cortland. Neither Mills nor Thomas, however, would admit to having been retained. Horace said nothing.[24]

The grand jury sat for over two days. The public was rather disappointed in that there was no open trial to report, and had to make do with scraps of news about the number of witnesses called. During the Grand Jury term two of Grace's sisters visited Chester in the jail. "Visit" is probably an inappropriate term since Chester had not asked to see *them*. One was the older sister Ada, whose house Chester had visited when he first met Grace. Chester claimed not to recognize Ada, something which caused many tongues to say "I told you so." although it wasn't quite apparent why.[25]

By the end of August the grand jury reported. To no one's surprise, Chester was indicted on a charge of murder in the first degree. The indictment was almost an anticlimax—the public had wanted something more to show for the month of heady stories that had now melted down to formal legal announcements.[26]

One small surprise did come out of the grand jury, though it held more meaning for Cortland readers than for the locals in Herkimer. Chester claimed that he had no means with which to provide for a legal defense, and asked the appointment of Senator Mills and Charles Thomas as defense attorneys. The court agreed and appointed the two men, expenses to be paid by the county.[27]

With this, the Gillette case almost disappeared from sight for over a month. September was a time for the public appetite to linger on baseball. It was Chicago's year. Both teams won pennants. When Herkimer residents gathered in front of the newspaper office to follow the telegraphed reports of the world series, they learned that Chicago's new American league team won. But Chester missed all this. He languished in his cell as the hot summer days cooled and October neared.

Public interest then turned to the coming gubernatorial election. William Randolph Hearst, the famous and wealthy publisher was running for governor of New York State as a

Democrat. He was opposed by a Republican reform candidate, Charles Evans Hughes. Across the street from Chester's jail cell George Ward's minor candidacy was remarkably visible.

Chester's lawyers really started working in October—late and for what amounted to minimum wages. Senator Mills waffled, and even considered withdrawing from the case, but in the end he stayed with Chester. He was, however, far from optimistic of his chances. After watching the ballyhoo of the past four months he was dour, or at best realistic, when he said that he had:

> ... no particular desire to appear in the Gillette Case because ... it had been made practically impossible for the case to be tried in Herkimer County owing to the sentimental way in which the press has handled the case . . .To my mind the press has rendered it practically impossible for an impartial jury to be secured in this county.[28]

There was an air of futility in Senator Mills' statement. The evidence and the work of the press made victory almost impossible to attain. Mills now appeared to feel that an unbiased trial was virtually unobtainable. Worse, he made no reference to any request for change of venue. November was coming and with it Chester's trial. As the first panel of names was drawn for jury use, Chester's lawyers finally went to work but they were far from enthusiastic.

jury (jö'ri), n.; pl. juries (-riz). [Early mod. E. jurie, < ME. jurie, < OF. juree, an oath, a judicial inquest, a jury (F. jury, jurt, < E.), < ML. jurata, a jury, a sworn body of men, orig. fem. pp. of L. jurare () F. jurer = Sp. Pg. jurar = It. giurare), swear, bind by an oath, < jus (jur-), law: see just.] 1. A certain number of men selected according to law, and sworn to inquire into or to determine facts concerning a cause or an accusation submitted to them, and to declare the truth according to the evidence adduced. Trial by jury signifies the determination of facts in the administration of civil or criminal justice by the arbitrament of such a body of men, subject to the superintendence of a judge, who directs the proceedings, decides what evidence is proper to be laid before the jury, and determines questions of law. The juries in the or-

11

TRIAL
BY JURY

With the election over, Herkimer girded for the approaching trial. Citizens sensed that an historic event was coming. Few realized, however, just how much their little city was to be transformed in the month to come. Preparation was the order of the day.

Trial had been set for the Monday following election day and local hotels began to book new guests shortly after the returns were in. Several of the witnesses were from out of town and began to arrive on the weekend. Many stayed at the Palmer House. If it lacked the style of its Chicago namesake, at least it sounded like the big time.[1]

Newspapers from as far away as Albany and Syracuse sent their own reporters. Many commuted to Herkimer by train. Express trains did not stop in Herkimer, however, and some chose to install themselves in local hotels. There was no alternative for the out-of-town press. They had to seek lodgings. Needless to say Herkimer bulged with visitors. Locals were slightly awed by the influx of strangers.

The previous week had been taken up with the fall elections. Hughes defeated Hearst for the governor's chair and in Herkimer George Ward won the judge's post. Little had appeared about the Gillette case during the election week and now the papers made up for the omission.

Detailed summaries were printed, retelling the whole story from the drowning to Chester's ordeal in jail. The small courthouse was ill equipped to handle the needs of the press corps and changes were hastily made. Both Western Union and Postal Telegraph, giants of the telegraph services, installed transmitting stations inside the courthouse. Each company had its operators ready to pound out copy from desks that were only a short distance from the courtroom.[2]

Trial opened on November 12th, a Monday. The second floor courtroom was crowded and even the balcony was occupied. People of the region knew that the first days of the trial would be procedural ones, yet the curious gathered almost from the start. Many wanted to see Chester. Some hoped to catch glimpses of Grace's parents and sisters who were in town as witnesses and who would probably be spectators as well. Some merely wished to rub shoulders with the growing body of the press. Herkimer had never seen anything like it.[3]

Judge Irving Devendorf opened the trial with an eye to the growing crowds. A liberal number of court attendants had been appointed ahead of time and he soon added more. George Ward stood ready to handle the case for the state. Chester did not appear for the opening session, but his attorneys, Senator Mills and Charles Thomas spoke for him.[4]

The Herkimer County Courthouse

114

The first major business was the jury. In 1906 New York State was still a long way from universal suffrage, and a large panel—all men— had been drawn earlier. On a last minute note of pessimism a second panel of names had been drawn and Monday opened with a room full of potential jurors. The composition of the jury was vital to both defense and prosecution and before Monday had passed it was clear that it would be several days before a jury was finally empaneled.

Each side had at its disposal thirty preemptive challenges. That is, each could dismiss without reason a potential juror and could do it on thirty different occasions. Neither however, wished to use up its preemptives during a long, drawn out battle. Each questioned potential jurors at length, hoping that it could persuade the judge to dismiss a candidate for "cause," thus saving another of its valuable preemptive tools.[5]

The number of men in the jury box varied all week long as each side allowed candidates to sit temporarily, subject to a later challenge. Ward attempted to exclude jurors who admitted to bias against capital punishment. Neither did he care to empanel jurors who had sons of Chester's age. Thomas, who did most of the questioning for the defense, probed into the family history of candidates. He did not care for jurors who had daughters of Grace's age.[6]

One by one the positions were filled as the week dragged on. Ed Curtis of Illion was accepted. His wife's cousin was Carrie Gleason, who had spoken to Chester in the jail.[7] It was a visit he probably knew nothing about and he sat back in the jury box with only a few companions, the twelve chairs and large spittoon. The press was speculating that jury selection might take a week. The jurors wondered how much longer it would take once the trial really commenced.

The press was right. Both sides chipped away at potential jurors with infinite care. On the other side of the railing the courtroom was filling with spectators. They were beginning to see what they had come for. Chester, when he finally arrived, was everything that the spectators and the press had expected. Reporters quickly put on the wire details of his dress (suit with wing collar), his stance (legs crossed) and his demeanor (he chewed gum constantly).[8]

By Wednesday Mr. and Mrs. Brown arrived in Herkimer. They were swamped with reporters. Mrs. Brown was bitter. Newspaper stories were already suggesting a romance between Chester and Harriet Benedict and Grace's mother claimed that as the reason for

Chester's doing away with her daughter. By Friday, with but eight in the jury box, the spectators were attracted to the sight of Grace's oldest sister in the crowd. Ada was holding a baby in her arms—the new baby that Grace had seen during her April vacation.[9]

Jury selection dragged on and became boring. Reporters pressed their interviews with potential witnesses. Some out-of-town reporters engaged in invention when things became dull. One distant newspaper claimed that Chester had attempted to escape from the courtroom. Thomas and Mills were incensed. Their client, the story implied, was acting as if guilty. But Ward and Judge Devendorf were angered too. False stories such as this reflected on the ability of the county to maintain order at the trial.[10]

With week's end it was necessary to pull names for another panel. The first two had been exhausted and the box was still not full. The selection was down to the last juror and this time the panel was from the city area alone. It was hoped that the last position could be filled in a matter of hours.

During the course of questioning the court excused one Charles Ward, a Sherman Klock and a man named R. M. Devendorf. Whether these men were related in any way to trial principals is not known, but in this Mohawk Valley area whose settlement began before the Revolution, family names, and especially the names of

The Jury

Palatine Germans were repeated by distant cousins up and down the river.[11]

By dusk on Friday the bored reporters began to sense that progress was finally being made. The jury needed one more man. Court was recessed for the night and on Saturday morning both sides worked vigorously to fill the last seat. By mid morning they had succeeded. It had taken five days and three panels of prospective jurors.[12]

Ed Curtis now found himself a full fledged member of a jury. Yet the twelve "good men and true" were not necessarily Chester's peers in every sense. To begin with, the law excluded all women. Of the men who had been chosen, most were farmers, although there was at least one clerk, one mechanic and one substitute mailman.

Most of the men were in their thirties and at least two were over sixty. Lastly, most were local in the sense that they lived close to the city of Herkimer. The most distant juror was W. L. Thayer of Russia, only seventeen miles away. The lightly populated north where the death had occurred was not represented at all.[13]

With a full jury box the trial was ready to proceed. Some expected that the actual trial would begin on Monday morning. In 1906, however, Saturday was a work day. Moreover there was pressure on the court to get this very expensive trial going. Ward was more than willing. He was ready to open for the State.

The district attorney wasted no time, but swung into his opening remarks with vigor. He first addressed the jurors themselves, pointing out the care with which they had been selected. He stressed that they had been chosen because they showed that they could make decisions based on evidence.

He dwelt for several minutes over the nature of the charge— murder in the first degree—and explained the difference between a crime of passion and premeditated murder where the crime was planned in advance and then carried out. This case was "something different" and "entirely apart from a blow that is struck or shot that is fired in sudden anger."

Ward then gave short verbal sketches of the two principal actors in the case. His description of Grace was that of an innocent young girl who came from a farm environment to work in a Cortland factory, met Chester and grew to love him. "In the end," Ward said, "she gave him all the treasures which she had."

Chester was described as the well traveled and knowledgeable young man who had seen the world. Ward was careful to stress Chester's manhood:

The idea will be carefully—has been carefully urged upon your minds while this jury was being drawn that he was somewhat of a boy. It is not true; he is a bearded man.

Ward feared that the public had already begun to view Chester as a young boy, and indeed the press was using the word repeatedly. Ward wished to make it clear to the jury. Chester was old enough to shave—and did.

The state then plunged into a detailed account of the fatal Adirondack vacation. Ward's expensive investigations now paid off handsomely, for he related in fine detail each and every move Chester had made while taking Grace through the mountains by rail. He left no doubt that every detail would be backed up by a very live witness in the days to come.

The district attorney was particularly careful to point out the manner in which Chester had registered at the various hotels, using pseudonyms until his appearance at Inlet. Stressed, too, was the fateful package of laundry. Ward slowly and patiently pointed out that Charles Gordon who left the laundry in Utica expected to pick it up at Old Forge later in the week when he would again be Chester Gillette.

Ward reached a climax when his story took the two young people out on the lake. He painted a picture of Chester striking the defenseless girl before she plunged into the lake. And then the district attorney dropped a quiet bomb in the little courtroom:

When her last death cry rang out over the waters of the lake, there was a witness to that and she will be here.

George Ward, who had been so generous with the press as to provide them with details of his evidence weeks in advance had seemingly held back one exotic bit of information. The press rattled the telegraph wires. An eyewitness would surely lock up the case for the State.

The State ended its opening with an account of Chester's leaving the scene of the crime and spending two days in the Fulton Chain enjoying the comforts of a resort hotel. Having outlined the story his witnesses would prove with their testimony, Ward concluded:

Now the court is going to adjourn this noon, and I have outlined these things sufficiently so that you will be prepared to hear the evidence. The only question you will have to decide, the only question that any honest or fair man has got to decide is whether

118

these witnesses whom you will hear here tell the truth. There is no other question in the case.[14]

Spectators went away looking forward to the following week. It would be an exciting trial. There would be a veritable parade of witnesses including, apparently, a surprise eyewitness.

There was even more. That weekend portions of Grace's letters were "made known." How or why they were leaked to the public remains a mystery. By Monday newspapers had printed what were alleged to be lines from her letters. While the general tenor of the excerpts rang true, the words did not.

If you fail to keep your promise, Chester, to come to me . Saturday, I will surely come to Cortland and you will have to see me there. I cannot possibly wait any longer.	. . .I am awfully sorry, but I have planned on Saturday and shall be in Cortland that night unless you meet me. I am awfully sorry but I cant [sic] help matters now. . .
You remember, Chester, that you told me once that you would never come back to this section until my dead body was brought back.	. . .I don't suppose I will be home for some time will I? Maybe not until I am sent home dead. You know, dear, you promised me that. . .

Newspaper accounts of November 17th purporting to be Grace's letters (left)[15] compared with Grace's original words (right).[16]

Ward, himself, would hardly have been a party to such a disclosure. The time for publicity had passed. Prior release of the letters, even in part, could have been considered prejudicial in the coming days when the district attorney wished to use them as evidence.

Clerks in his office, however, may have recounted passages from memory for the benefit of friendly reporters. By the time that newsmen had cast them into print Grace's words had passed through two or three levels of recall and suffered badly.

Monday saw the beginning of the second week of the trial. For most of the public this was the *real* trial which was about to begin. Now they were going to see evidence and witnesses. Over a thousand people crowded into the small courtroom, using the balcony as well as the spectator portion of the main floor. They sensed that Ward would produce a dramatic trial and they were not disappointed.

119

The State had barely begun to establish its case when Ward sought to introduce as evidence the letters written between Grace and Chester. The defense lawyers jumped up to protest that the letters were inadmissible. After a long harangue Judge Devendorf made a decision. The letters could be used by the State, but "only for the purpose of showing how the deceased regarded her relationship with the defendant." Facts mentioned in the letters were to be disregarded! Chester's attorneys challenged the decision but Devendorf remained adamant. The letters could be used.[17]

This was the stuff the public had been seeking! Even more elated was the working press. Weekend rumors betrayed the fact that the reporters knew a great deal about the now famous letters. One reporter knew even more. Edith Cornwall reported for the Syracuse *Herald* and she was the kind of reporter that lived for the great "scoop."

Somewhere during the weekend Cornwall had discovered that Ward was, indeed, going to introduce the letters—on Monday. Assuming that the press would devour (and print) every word of the documents, Ward made an effort to assure that the public would receive an accurate copy of the letters read at the trial and not merely a stenographic copy scribbled from the press seats. He had four copies of the letters typed up from the handwritten originals.

One of these copies was for Ward to read in the courtroom. A second was for the Associated Press and the third for the United Press. Individual newspapers would have to deal with the two great press associations. But Edith Cornwall discovered the existence of that fourth copy and skillfully obtained it for her own use. Reporters of the day were willing to part with a few dollars to obtain a beat on their opponents.

On Monday morning Cornwall had the means of obtaining that advantage. She could send the text of the letters directly to the *Herald* In Syracuse by wire but before the session began the letters were still not public documents. Not until they had been read on the floor of the court would they fall into the public domain. Should the defense succeed in barring the letters they could not be printed in the afternoon paper.

The feisty reporter was almost certain that they would be available, but she could not guarantee it. She then hedged her bets and went to the telegrapher at the local rail station. She asked him to get the *Herald* on the wire and hold them until word came that the letters could be used.

The operator could not hold an open wire for a private party and said so. But Cornwall had tricks up her sleeve. She gave the telegrapher a copy of the New York State constitution—that was long enough to occupy anyone for half a day—and guaranteed that the *Herald* would pay for the bill. The old brasspounder merely had to start sending text.

In the meantime, Cornwall had cornered a messenger boy and told him to stand by at the courthouse. When Ward stood up to read the first of the letters, the Syracuse reporter sent her messenger racing to the railroad station with the order to start sending the *Herald* copy. That evening Syracuse readers had the letters and read them one by one. Edith Cornwall had struck again![18]

They learned, too, what a dramatic session that morning had been in the crowded courtroom. By the time that Ward had finished the last of Grace's impassioned letters the courtroom was bursting with emotion. Tears flowed copiously. The press claimed that even hardened reporters broke down and cried. This last may have been sheer hyperbole, but the public found itself caught up in the story.[19]

Readers took to heart Grace's last letter and its farewell to her childhood home. It was the very letter which Lizzie Crain had found in Chester's room.

The press associations had done their job well. From coast to coast the American reader began to absorb the Gillette Case. In New York City the Thaw case was mired in legal maneuvering. In Herkimer the real trial had only just begun.

12

THE TRIAL CONTINUES

ATTORNEY THOMAS   CHESTER GILLETTE

Each day the courtroom was crowded to the doors. If the public appetite had been whetted by hearing the letters, it now hungered for a glimpse of the principals and Ward obliged. As Monday wore on he called to the witness stand Chester's landlady, his uncle, working companions and even Ada Hawley, Grace's sister. Each had his own anecdote of Chester's months in Cortland.[1]

Among the witnesses to arrive in Herkimer was Harriet Benedict who was accompanied by her father, the Cortland attorney. The press had received word that the prosecution would attempt to establish a romantic link between Chester and Harriet. The more sensational sheets had already printed stories about a full blown romance while the upstate papers which considered themselves bastions of conservative journalism wrote about their more flamboyant rivals. In either case the public was beginning to hear a great deal about Hattie Benedict.

Hattie came prepared. She was preceded by a statement issued to the press:

> I wish to state to my friends and general public, through the press that I have never been engaged to Chester E. Gillette, now on trial for murder in Herkimer County; that our acquaintance was of but a limited duration and that not a word or suggestion was ever made between us of such relations.
>
> I have never communicated with or received a word from him since his arrest. Neither myself nor either of my parents has ever visited him in jail nor have I ever sent him flowers or candy as has been reported in certain papers.

I have not been at the trial since its commencement and it is absolutely untrue that I sat in the courtroom by his lawyers as has been reported.

I call upon all newspapers to cease publication of these false stories circulated about me.

I am advised to hold all newspapers to strict accountability for publishing any libelous articles concerning me.

Harriet P. Benedict,
Cortland, Nov 17, 1906[2]

The Benedicts were angry and the hand of Hattie's father showed in the last paragraph of the document.

But Ward obliged the press and entered this new and tantalizing territory. He brought forth the register from the Raymond House—the book that Harriet Benedict had treated so playfully on the Fourth. That simple book had become an official document and bore a new label—exhibit 30. There in Hattie's handwriting were the telltale words:

Harriet Benedict, New York City
Chester Gillette, San Francisco[3]

The district attorney was attempting to create a love triangle out of Chester, Grace and Harriet. Harriet had been subpoenaed and her presence on the witness list had already fueled many rumors.

Ward's questions were almost unnecessary. The book raised questions of its own. Why did Chester take Harriet Benedict out on a holiday when Grace was home and pregnant? Why were the names linked to false addresses?

Hattie took the stand and calmly explained while the press watched every expression on her face. Her statements were clear and firm. She knew Chester only slightly. She had been out with him on only two or three previous occasions. Only once had she sent him a post card and that to remind him of a poster he had promised and never sent.

The entries in the Raymond register were innocent enough. All the young people played games with the book. There was no need for dinner guests to register. It was merely youthful fun.[4]

Her answers—helped out by cross examination—seemed to explain everything. Harriet was a good witness and Ward never managed to push the theory of a rich sweetheart any further than this. Yet, as always, there were those who went away muttering "Where there's smoke there's fire!" Harriet would never be allowed to forget her small role in the Gillette story.

The trial, now at its midpoint, was attracting attention throughout the country. More and more wire service stories were printed in communities that had never heard of Cortland or Herkimer.

In the next county to the north farmer William J. Griffin joined the hordes of interested readers. The St. Lawrence County farmer lived only forty miles from the death site, but no road connected his farm community with Big Moose across the Adirondack foothills. Still, proximity provided a link, if only a slender one, with the country's most sensational trial.

Griffin was an avid reader, but one who considered the uproar to be a matter of yellow journalism. His only passions were politics and agriculture. Yet interest in the Griffin household rose rapidly as the trial progressed. It followed the proceedings in the newspaper which came by mail three times a week.

On alternate days Griffin, possibly prompted by the women of the house, walked three miles to Oswegatchie village to buy a current paper. In an age before radio and television the public was spared the benefit of "instant" bulletins. No matter that the news was a day old when the paper arrived. To people like the Griffins it was as fresh as the morning milk. The family never missed a day of the trial.[5]

From Utica to Little Falls people by the hundreds wanted more than the written word. Locals strove to visit the crowded courtroom at least once so that they could say in future years that they had been there.

The crowd was great and the public understood little of the game of adversaries unfolding on the other side of the railing. To them it mattered only that they could see the principals in action. They ogled the judge and court officers. Even a stranger quickly distinguished between Ward at the prosecutor's table and the two defense attorneys. The twelve men in the jury box were mortals like the spectators themselves and some visitors knew a juror or two.

On their own side of the rail spectators watched the men and women of the press and their messengers. These people wrote and drew rapidly as if they feared that they might miss some momentous word should they suffer the slightest lapse. There were other notables among the lay people. Members of the Brown family were often there and spectators pointed them out to one another.

But the big prize was Chester. To the press and visitors alike he was the attraction. Not that Chester openly sought it. He normally

125

looked straight ahead and showed little emotion. Indeed, that was the thing that fascinated the public. Before their very eyes Chester sat and listened stoically to the long, horrid story that unfolded each day, yet his facial expression rarely changed.

Interest in the witnesses varied. The public, and the press too, had already begun to choose favorites. They had found the early witnesses only moderately interesting and certainly not exciting. Harriet Benedict had been a different matter. The public was primed for romance even if they did not get it.

Now Ward turned to the fatal trip in the Adirondacks. The witnesses who followed testified about Chester's sojourn north-ward with Grace. Their testimony was usually brief and to the point and the gallery knew just what it implied. Many of these witnesses were from Herkimer County and known to the courtroom spectators.

Ralph Weaver who had been desk clerk at the Tabor House in DeRuyter in July identified Chester, but as Charles George from New York City who had taken a room on the night of July eighth. With a page from the hotel register in his hands Weaver showed how "George" was listed for a seven o'clock call next morning. Other witnesses placed Grace and Chester in the hotel and on the streets of DeRuyter on the ninth of July.[6]

Both Josephine Patrick and Gladys Westcott were called. These students testified to knowing Chester in the year prior to the trip. On occasion they had been together socially. Both placed Chester on the train that left DeRuyter for Canastota on the ninth. Josephine Patrick repeated the details of the conversation with Chester on the train. Ward was particularly looking for her statement that Chester had asked where the girls would be in the Adirondacks. Upon finding that they would be in the Fulton Chain he promised to drop by as early as Friday of that week. The two witnesses were clear on one point. Chester was alone in the car. He seemed to have had no companion on the train.[7]

Ward carefully called his witnesses in the order of events. John Pallas came from Canastota. He worked as a New York Central station agent there and could identify Chester. He was the young man who had purchased a mileage book at his ticket window in July.[8]

William Martin the owner of the Hotel Martin in Utica was called as was the man who had been desk clerk on July ninth. Each testified to seeing Chester in the hotel with a young woman. As he had done in the case of the Tabor House, Ward brought forth a page of the hotel register. The former clerk identified the page and Chester as the young man who had signed it, but as Charles Gorden.[9]

Guy Zimerman also appeared from Utica. He was the laundry employee who had accepted Chester's laundry and promised to forward the clean clothing to Old Forge later in the week.[10]

From Tupper Lake came Myron Newman, owner of Alta Cliff Cottage, and his employee Clara Greenwood. Also summoned was Dan McDonald the driver who had taken the couple from the rail station to the Alta Cliff. All three placed the couple in the Alta Cliff for the night of July tenth. The young witness told her tale of Grace bursting into tears and throwing her arms around the waitress when she broke down in the dining room.[11]

Royal Fuller, a newsman from New York City testified to seeing the couple on the train and later at the Glennmore hotel. James McAllister came down from Big Moose to tell how he had driven the pair to the hotel and how they had given him post cards to mail. Curiously, Ward called various postal clerks to testify that these cards had passed through their hands. At this point many observers may have begun to consider Ward's thoroughness a matter of overkill.[12]

The story was now on familiar ground. They had read and reread accounts of the fatal visit to the Glennmore on Big Moose Lake and many knew the area well. Andrew Morrison, the proprietor of the Glennmore told in detail of the arrival of the couple at his hotel and how Chester toyed with the idea of taking a steamboat ride. In what had become a ritual, Ward produced the hotel register with Chester's fateful entry:

Carl Grahm, Albany
Grace Brown, South Otselic[13]

Morrison's father, Robert Morrison, testified that he was the operator of the boat livery on the water. It was he who had rented the rowboat to Chester and watched the couple row off toward the East in the late morning. Ward then brought in several summer cottagers who had seen the rowboat meander along the southern shore that July day.[14]

The audience, reporters and public alike, were now poised for Ward's coup de grace. In his opening statement the district attorney had promised that he would produce a witness to Grace's death cry. Now, however, he fell short of his promise. His witness, Marjory Carey of East Orange, N. J., could only report that she had heard a scream across the lake at the dinner hour. She had seen nothing.[15]

Most of the watchers were disappointed. They had wanted an eye witness. But Chester's attorneys breathed more easily. To date there had been no witness to the death itself. The evidence that was given by each witness this week was damaging but none of it shed light on the events in the rowboat. No one yet *knew* what had happened.

Ward quickly pushed on past the moment of Grace's death. He called hotel personnel from the places where Chester had stayed and had eaten on the Fulton Chain Lakes. The minister from Lowville, Mr. Dean, was called along with his daughter and both recounted the climb on Black Bear Mountain. Captain Hoffman of the mail boat went over Chester's request to collect his laundry at Old Forge.[16]

If, at first, the audience and jury felt that this testimony was drawn out and irrelevant Ward quickly made it clear that it was, indeed, significant—even damning. He was pointing to an unanswered question that hovered over the room. If the drowning *had* been an accident, how could Chester have immersed himself so easily in the carefree life of a tourist in the forty eight hours that followed?

Captain Hoffman's testimony was also a reminder that Chester had planned on being on the Fulton Chain late in the fatal week, and under his own name at that. The press community was of the opinion that things were closing in on Chester.

The state's case was grinding toward a climax. The routine of the court was now becoming the routine of the community as well. The courtroom which had been crowded in the early days was now jammed to capacity. Experienced spectators arrived early and those who could not enter were left to mill about in the street between the courthouse and the jail. More than one newspaper printed stories about threats against Chester which had been made in the street.[17]

If the crowds outside the courthouse were unruly and restless, those inside were learning to cope with the routine of the court. They arrived early and saved seats for others. Many came with friends and relatives. Some even brought children so that the child could later say that he had been present at the famous trial.

As the ritual went on and seats became harder to get the wise ones brought lunches. They had learned that during the luncheon recess others would take the seats that they had worked so hard to acquire earlier in the day. A picnic atmosphere arose in the empty courtroom after the officers of the court adjourned to more proper dining establishments.

By late in the second week the combination of closely packed bodies and warm food began to reach the bench. Judge Devendorf finally ordered the courtroom cleared after the morning session. The windows were to be thrown open and the room aired. Picnic time was over.[14]

By now Ward had called over seventy witnesses and was fulfilling the prophecy of those who had predicted that this would be the most expensive trial in Herkimer's history.

But not all of this expense stemmed from the cost of witnesses. Ward compiled an extensive list of trial exhibits—101 in all—and used them dramatically. If there was no eyewitness there would at least be a mass of physical evidence with which to bombard Chester.

The state's first exhibit was a map, a large scale map of Big Moose Lake. It was placed in the courtroom the morning that the Ward opened his case and remained for most of the trial.[19]

The letters written between Grace and Chester were among the most famous exhibits and by the day after their introduction it was certain that every spectator in the room had read their contents in the newspapers. Now they lay on the evidence table, small bundles of paper too far from the spectators to read but heavy with suggestion. The pages taken from the various hotel registers lay there too, and like the letters looked insignificant except for what the public knew was written on them.

The district attorney brought to the courtroom Chester's tennis racket, his suitcase, his camera, the tripod and the clothes in which Chester had traveled to Inlet. Prominent among Chester's things was exhibit 37, the package of laundry that had been forwarded to Old Forge.

Brought into the room too, was Grace's trunk and the clothes she had carefully packed for the Adirondack trip. More heart-rending were the things she had worn on the last day. They were all there, carefully itemized down to two separate pieces of garter now handed over by the district attorney and given the numbers 95 and 96.[20]

Exhibit 88 was awesomely large. Ward had ordered that the boat be removed from the lake and crated. It was then shipped by rail to Herkimer. Now it was brought into the courtroom, and placed in the crowded space between the bench and the railing. In that confined space it looked much larger than it was. On the firm floor it seemed sturdy and unlikely to tip over. With the boat were the oars that had been recovered floating nearby.[21]

Perhaps the most delicate of all exhibits was number 92, a lock of hair caught in the gunwale of the boat. The emotions of the spectators, if not the jury, were stirred by this relic of the past. It was compared with a similar lock that had been saved in South Otselic at an earlier date when Grace's sister had cut her hair. There was little point in either exhibit since the identity of the dead girl was never questioned. It did, however, heighten feeling in the courtroom.[22]

Among the later exhibits submitted by the state were notes from the post mortem examination. By today's standards they were sketchy and frightfully limited. These notes indicated that the fetus had been removed from the body and placed in a jar of formaldehyde. The very next exhibit was a sealed and covered package submitted by the doctor whose name appeared on the post mortem report. Reporters wasted little time in guessing the contents of the jar. Its presence did no more than feed an emotional flame.[23]

Ward's witnesses were now those who had been involved in the discovery of the body and the investigations which had followed. Men from the little steamboat Zylphia described the discovery and recovery of the body. There was no mention of the young boy, Roy Higby, who had been aboard. His family had carefully kept him from being called as a witness.[24]

Coroner Isaac Coffin told of his visit to Big Moose Lake to investigate the death. Shortly afterward Semour Getman of Frankfort was called. He was the undertaker who had gone to Big Moose Lake with Coroner Coffin on July 13th. Both Getman and Coffin noticed abrasions to the face, nose and mouth of the victim.[25]

Coffin's actions at Big Moose were both strange and contradictory. On the one hand he called for help from the county seat, expressing an opinion that there had been foul play. On the other, he released the body to Getman and allowed the undertaker to transport it back to his establishment in Frankfort. In short order Getman had injected the body with embalming fluid. On the next day a panel of physicians visited the undertaker's workrooms to conduct a post mortem investigation.

At the trial these doctors were called one after another and each agreed to the accuracy of the autopsy report which had been filed. The evidence they gave was not overwhelming and, indeed, the defense noted several points that would leave the report open to question. Modern attorneys would ask even more probing questions.

How competent were these physicians to conduct a detailed post mortem examination? All were local doctors but none was a specialist in forensic medicine. Why had Getman been permitted to work on the body before the examination? Why was the report so sketchy? The conclusion of the autopsy was a one line summary stating that the cause of death was "Primarily concussion, followed by syncope and then asphyxiation."[26]

The autopsy, though brief, was enough for Ward. Damage *had* been done to the girl's head prior to death, although there was some question that it was the actual cause of death. The several doctors who had conducted the autopsy, however, thought that injury to the head was the decisive factor.

The defense lawyers reached high points of anger. Whether death was caused by a blow to the head by the defendant as the state claimed, or during the process of falling out of the boat as the defense insisted, was unknown. There was still no witness to that one critical moment on the lake.

Ward turned the screws again. He asked to introduce the covered jar that had come from the post mortem. The defense objected. Chester's attorneys pointed out to the court that they would admit freely to the fact that Grace had been pregnant rather than display the bottled fetus before the entire court. Such a move would certainly be prejudicial and would appeal to public emotion. Ward had won a point. The jar was as telling when covered as it was open. He could close his case with satisfaction. There may have been no witness to the crime but the level of feeling against Chester was running very, very high.[27]

JUSTICE DEVENDORF

13

TO THE VERDICT

By the time that Ward brought the prosecution case to an end the trial was well into the third week. The public was eager to see what kind of defense Mills and Thomas would attempt. Before Chester's lawyers could start their own case, however, Ward pulled another string *outside* the courtroom.

In New York City the defense lawyers for Harry Thaw had considered a plea of "Not guilty by reason of insanity." This was a new and novel approach in that age and Thaw, himself, fought the idea. But Ward feared that the Gillette defense might follow that very route in Herkimer. Accordingly, Ward planned a sanity test in the jail. The prosecution asked Chester if he would cooperate and the young man agreed.[1] Where were Chester's lawyers at this critical moment?

Ward brought three alienists, as psychiatrists were then called, to Herkimer and proceeded to test Chester's faculties. If forensic medicine in 1906 was in its formative years, psychiatry had barely appeared on the scene. Chester was besieged with questions and many referred to his family. At that time it was widely believed that all mental illness was hereditary.

Chester's grandfather was thought to have been "mentally weak," although the source of this allegation was never stated. Chester's father was taken to task in absentia. After all, he had been a Dowieite. Ward would have done well to avoid this topic when supporting Chester's sanity. The Dowie movement sat poorly with most Easterners and there was a rumor that Chester's father had given over the family furnishings to that religious sect.

Ward's three experts skirted the Gillette parentage and went straight to the problem—Chester. They quietly entered the jail and asked the young man a battery of questions. It was never clear whether this secrecy was to protect Chester from public ridicule or to hide the examination from the defense attorneys.

Following the oral sessions Chester was subjected to clinical examination. The three experts administered a "needle test." There was an obscure belief that in some cases of insanity one side of the body was more sensitive to pain than the other. To test for this, needles were jabbed into the young man from both left and right. Presumably Chester was equally sensitive for nothing more was said.

Then the alienists blindfolded the patient and dropped a flatiron on his foot. Chester's reaction was most predictable and the experts promptly certified him as sane. Ward immediately released all the details to reporters. Whatever Mills and Thomas may have thought, they did not attempt an insanity plea.[2]

When their turn came Mills and Thomas faced a dilemma. In American criminal law the burden of proof is supposed to lie with the state. But after Ward's long, thorough and almost overwhelming presentation the roles seemed to be reversed. There was now a burden on the defense to do *something* to counter the prosecution case. The problem was that much, and perhaps most, of the state's case was true and it was locked in by solid testimony. In many areas the defense readily admitted the allegations:

Chester *had* been Grace's lover.
He *had* been seeing other girls.
He *had* taken Grace on a trip to the Adirondacks.
He *had* used false names.
He *had* taken Grace out in a rowboat.
He *had* been with her when she died.
He *had* walked away from the lake.
He *had* assumed his own identity again.
He *had* sought money and his laundry through arrangements made before the death.

But Chester adhered to his claim that he had *not* struck the girl or caused her drowning. So much that had appeared in print and which had been spoken in the courtroom was true that the public wondered how Chester could claim that this one bit was not. The defense was forced to attempt the negative proof—that something had *not* happened. But how could this be done?

Senator Mills,
leader of the defense team

Senator Mills took center stage for the defense and even before its case was opened he attempted a legal ploy. He asked that the court dismiss the charges and release Chester for a variety of reasons. The evidence given had been insufficient to prove guilt beyond a reasonable doubt. Other evidence, unfavorable to the prosecution had been suppressed.

No one expected that these requests would receive serious consideration from Judge Devendorf, but Mills made one strong attempt to combat the mass of the district attorney's attack. He asked that the case be dismissed because of error in the state's case. Specifically, Mills referred to Ward's promise to produce a witness to the fatal moment. The witness who testified had actually seen nothing.[3]

The defense motion was denied.

Thomas opened for the defense and made a long address. Again he noted the "error" in the state's case and the fact that there had been no eyewitness to the alleged crime. He, too, promised to bring a witness later—a doctor who had seen the body shortly after its removal from the water.

But the first witness for the defense was Chester, himself. This was a calculated risk. The state was sure to be rigorous in its cross examination. On the other hand, Chester's actions had been recounted in the courtroom in fine detail. Little could be lost by allowing Chester to tell his own story. Everyone—and certainly the jury—was eager to hear *his* version.

Chester was sworn in and commenced to give his account of the tragic trip that ended in Big Moose Lake.[4] His treatment of the boat rental and the row along the south shore agreed in most respects with the testimony of the many state witnesses several days before. The courtroom was hushed when he finally came to the critical moment late in the afternoon.

After picnicking on the shore he and Grace had gone out in the boat for the final time. At long last they began to talk out their common problem. Grace wanted to continue on to Fourth Lake. Chester thought it was time to return to South Otselic and confess all to Grace's parents. Grace protested. She could not face her parents.

Chester insisted and then, without warning, Grace jumped over the side of the boat. There was confusion. Chester attempted to help. (It was no secret to anyone in the courtroom that Grace could not swim.) But as Chester attempted to effect a rescue the boat overturned. When he surfaced there was no sign of Grace. He never saw her again.

When Chester reached shore and found his suitcase full of dry clothes, panic set in. In fear he picked up his belongings and started walking away from the terrible scene. He threw the umbrella away and later hid the tennis racket under a log. Chester's story was not without logic, but the public knew that Ward was waiting in the wings with his own questions for Chester. Attendance at the trial was still full and more than ever were turned away each day.

Chester's testimony as a defense witness was finished by Wednesday noon. That afternoon the district attorney began his cross examination. It was an ordeal and promised to get worse in the following session. Thursday was Thanksgiving Day, and Chester had a brief respite in his cell, complete with a Thanksgiving Dinner. But the public was avidly waiting for Friday to come. Their main concern was to see how Chester would stand up under the real cross examination. Many were expecting (and some were hoping) that he would crack.[5]

By Friday most of the participants were restless. Chester, no doubt, wished that the ordeal of the cross examination would go away. The spectators had largely made up their minds as to guilt and innocence. Meanwhile, the town's hotels were full of witnesses who had come expecting to remain in Herkimer for only two or three days. Now the trial was approaching the end of its third week. The witnesses chafed.

Ward circled for the kill. He did not spend as much time with Chester as some had predicted, but struck at the credibility of Chester's testimony. He wanted to know if Chester had gone over this story before. He had. With whom? His lawyers. How many times? Chester wasn't sure. Bit by bit Ward subtly introduced doubt—a suspicion that Chester's story of the trip and drowning was not spontaneous but carefully rehearsed for presentation in the courtroom.

The thrust of Ward's questioning was directed at the truth of Chester's account. The spectators (but possibly not the jury) recalled claims by the press that Chester had told other and varying tales during the July investigations. During Ward's presentation many people had raised questions about his uncorroborated account of the death scene. They were again visited by doubt—This time doubt about Chester's own story.[6]

Once Ward finished with the cross examination Mills and Thomas could recover control of the defense. But there was very little left to control. The remaining witnesses were all from Cortland and were in Herkimer to affirm Chester's character. It didn't take long.

Chester's character witnesses included the Presbyterian minister, a man from the *Cortland Standard* and several co-workers from the factory. They had little to add in direct testimony and tended to make embarrassing statements under cross examination.[7]

Two of these, Ella Hoag and Neva Wilcox had the dubious distinction of having been called by both prosecution and defense. Each worked in the factory and each seemed to tell more under Ward's cross examination than under direct.

Mrs. Hoag told of seeing Grace "Go to the window of the stockroom where Chester worked, though not very often." The reader of this newspaper transcription of her testimony was left to untangle the ambiguity for himself.[8]

In spite of the defense promise to produce a doctor as a witness, none materialized. In its own way the defense was as unfulfilling as the prosecution had been, just when key testimony was needed.

In the last hours of the trial several witnesses were recalled.

Chester had testified that under no circumstances had he asked to hire a horse in DeRuyter the night before meeting Grace. On recall John Coy owner of the Tabor House claimed that Chester, while posing as Charles George, attempted to hire a rig and asked directions to the Brown farm in South Otselic.[9]

To Ward this directly conflicting testimony was consistency itself. Chester, he claimed, had deliberately made the request knowing that it would be remembered later and would link the fictional Charles George with Grace Brown and her fatal trip to the Adirondacks. To Ward this meant premeditation.

It was almost over. Mills stood up to summarize. The defense case had not been strong and Mills now put all his effort into the summary, warning the jurors that under law there could be no conviction if a single doubt existed in their minds.[10]

Again he attacked the prosecution for its failure to provide the critical witness that Ward had promised. Mills also pointed out that the state had failed to prove that any plan of marriage had existed between Chester and Grace, in spite of suggestions to that effect. Similarly, while the state had implied, and the newspapers claimed, that Chester had become engaged to Harriet Benedict, there was not a shred of evidence to support it.

Finally he delivered a scathing attack on the medical testimony and the doctors who had given it. He scorned the way in which the state had allowed the undertaker to treat the body prior to a medical examination. The post mortem, itself, was reported on a single page of paper with no supporting work notes.

His attack on the physicians was particularly bitter. He knew all five doctors, yet castigated them for their role in the examination. Mills wasted no pity but charged them with omission, with parrot-like adherence to the same story and in a moment of anger used the word "graft." It was the strongest attack the courtroom had seen in the three weeks of the trial. He finished with:

> The district attorney will now present to you the other side of this case with all the prejudice and resentment that he can command.[11]

Ward summed up for the state and spoke for hours. If Mills' tone had been angry and vindictive, Ward replied in kind. He claimed that his opponent was desperate, else he would never have resorted to the shocking claims of fraud.

If Mills had taken Ward to task for not bringing a promised witness Ward returned the favor. He pointed out that Mills and Thomas had kept a doctor at the their table throughout the defense case. Not once, however, had they called this man to testify. They were afraid to.[12]

When Ward ended, the wrangling between the two lawyers was done. Judge Devendorf stated the charges and outlined the work of the jury. It was suppertime on Tuesday, December fourth when the jury was led away to begin its deliberation. This was the part in which the crowd could not participate. Still, it was rumored in the papers that the local betting odds were two to one that Chester would be convicted of no less than second degree murder.[13]

Few expected a verdict that evening. Much of the crowd left the courthouse. Newsmen lingered around the telegraphers filing color stories. Responding to a rising air of tension in the community, the authorities had recently increased the police coverage at the courthouse and in the street. Newsmen called it an armed camp.

Before midnight the jury returned. Court quickly reconvened and foreman Marshall Hatch rose to give the verdict—guilty of murder in the first degree.[14]

Fewer than five hundred spectators were left and they dispersed to discuss the new event. The jurors went home, but not before stopping at the Palmer House and paying their respects to Mr. and Mrs. Brown. Grace's mother received the news of the conviction with a mixture of elation and guilt that she should rejoice over such a terrible event.[15]

Chester's jailers hurried him across the street to the jail. He had just time to compose a telegram to his father. It was simple and to the point:

"Dear Father, I am convicted."[16]

Judge Devendorf set sentencing Thursday morning, less than two days away. Guards now watched Chester day and night. Before taking its next step the defense needed time to digest the trial transcript. But the clerks were slow and the huge document was still incomplete. Devendorf postponed sentencing until Monday, December 10th.

On that Monday morning Chester appeared in the court-room for the last time. His attorneys made one last attempt to have the verdict put aside. Then Devendorf closed the last legal door in Herkimer County and pronounced the sentence—that Chester be taken to Auburn prison and put to death by electrocution sometime in the week of December 28th.[17]

The public appetite was sated. Few disagreed, and many were pleased.

Entrance to the third floor cell area of the Herkimer County Jail where Chester was kept.

MOTHER'S EFFORTS AROUSE SYMPATHY

Mrs. Gillette Is Going Back to the Mountains of Colorado—Story of Her Struggle to Avert Execution of the Death Penalty.

14

THE WAITING TIME

During the weekend between the verdict and the sentence the press enjoyed its last great fling. *The Syracuse Herald* which had covered the trial in greater detail than any other daily now devoted an entire sixteen page Sunday supplement to a review of the Gillette Case. The cover of the tabloid-sized section was graced with a full page pen and ink profile of Chester.

The supplement was a compilation of Edith Cornwall's stories of the crime, including the letters from Grace to Chester. The foreword was written by Harold McGrath, a Syracuse writer and humorist, but his comments were severe and foreboding. They probably reflected very well the public temper of the day:

> It is hoped that no well meaning meddlers will importune the governor to forget his duty and pardon Gillette. Guiltless though he might be in one crime, he is guilty of another. . .[1]

Ironically, this special section carried a full page advertisement—a promotion for the paper's Christmas edition which was to come out the following week. It was an indication of things to come, for in a few more days the public would have to turn to other things for sensation. Chester's case was winding down.[2]

The one story that reporters desperately wanted was a confession. A confession would neatly tie up the package that had become a household term as the "Gillette Case." The press knew its business. The public which had an appetite for conviction and penalty, also thirsted for confession.

But Chester refused to cooperate. There was no confession. Still, during the course of the trial one report had painted a picture of Chester admitting all in the presence of his jailers. It was widely circulated and came off the press wires to appear in the Denver papers.

Mrs. Gillette who was following the newspaper accounts of the trial with friends in Denver sent Chester a telegram asking him to repent. Chester assumed that his mother had taken the news account at face value and presumed him to be guilty.

The jail officials (who may have been piqued at words having been put in *their* mouths) helped Chester wire an immediate rebuttal to Denver. There would be no confession before the sentencing—if ever.[3]

Louise Gillette could stay no longer in Denver. She secured a position with the *Denver Times* and the New York *American* to act as a writer and correspondent. This gave her transportation to Herkimer and she arrived there on the Sunday night after the conviction, too late to visit Chester. Next morning she managed to convince the jailers that she was, indeed, Chester's mother and met her son for the first time since he had come east, and the last before he was sentenced.

Chester's first question to his mother was: "How are the kids? Are they in school?"[4] His question strangely resembled the message Grace Brown had written on her last post card to South Otselic. Mrs. Gillette crossed the street and sat next to Senator Mills during the sentencing.

Because she was considered an exclusive writer for the two newspapers, Louise Gillette was difficult to interview. Reporters did receive a break from Chester. He agreed to be interviewed by the press the day after his sentence. Since only one person could enter the tiny cell in the county jail a pool arrangement was reached. The unanimous choice of the press corps was Edith Cornwall, and she climbed to the third floor for a face to face meeting with the condemned man.[5]

But not every newspaper exploited the Gillette case with impunity. As the trial blossomed into national prominence in November the *New York Morning Telegraph* had done its own feature on the upstate story.

Curiously, the editors sought out the paper's best known sports writer. He was given the assignment and a relatively blank check. But there was no visit to the trial—not even a trip to Herkimer. Everything was written in Manhattan.

142

The story was critical. The author raised serious questions about the ability of the defendant to receive a fair trial in Herkimer county. This twist was not totally new. While the *Telegraph* published its account other papers, including upstate journals, were giving out colorful descriptions of the crowds that surrounded the courthouse and the threats allegedly directed at Chester.

When copies of the *Telegraph* appeared in Herkimer a furor developed. County officials were incensed that a "big city" paper would infer that the county could not maintain order at the trial. Herkimer citizens were as angered as their elected officials, but for a different reason. The New York writer had the bad judgment to refer to Herkimer people as "bushmen." Something should be done.

Something was. Immediately after the close of the Gillette trial the Herkimer county court served warrants on two of the editors and the New York writer. One was too ill to travel, but the other two, including the writer, were taken to Herkimer County to account for their deeds.

The indictment accused the three men of violating section 143 of the New York State Penal Code. The locals cared little about the fineprint of the law, but they were intrigued by the size of their haul. It started:

> Supreme Court, County of Herkimer.
> The People of the State of New York
> vs.
> Henry N. Cary, W. E. Lewis and
> W. B. Masterson, alias Bat Masterson.[6]

The writer of the "bushman" line was none other than the famous "Bat" Masterson, the man who had been a marshal in the West, the man who had gone on to New York City and become writer of sports. In that age baseball was often limited to line scores in the papers. *Sports* meant boxing (often illegal) and horse racing. It was his more famous background as a lawman that had prompted the *Telegraph* to give him the Gillette story.

Masterson had become a real New Yorker. Friends said that after only a few years in the city he sounded and acted like a native. But he was still impetuous and was regularly involved in fights and brawls and this time he had taken on an entire county.

On December 17th Masterson, along with one of the editors appeared in the Herkimer courtroom. They were found guilty of printing stories about mobs when mobs did not exist. For this they were each fined fifty dollars. Herkimer was avenged. Masterson kept his thoughts to himself, but the small fine hardly hurt. To the contrary, notoriety was just the thing that Bat Masterson appreciated. He gloried in the attention.[7]

Chester's mother had little time to meet with her son after sentence was passed. In two short days Chester was taken by Undersheriff Klock and an assistant and slipped on board the 10:24 morning train to the west. No plans of the transfer were published and a low profile kept crowds of curious people to a minimum.

The little party traveled in a compartment of a Pullman car which carried the "Runaways," a traveling troupe of performers. The actors crowded around Chester for much of the way. He was particularly popular with the young women performers and most came away with slips of paper with Chester's signature for a souvenir.

In Auburn a crowd had gathered at the station. But by prior arrangement the train stopped at the Perrine Street grade crossing. Here the prisoner was transferred to a closed, horse-drawn conveyance and driven to the prison.[8]

The initial sentence had set a December date for execution, but Mills and Thomas immediately filed notice that they would lodge an appeal. The case would take time to prepare and only then could it be presented to the Court of Appeals, the highest court in New York State. Chester would remain in Auburn for 473 days.

Auburn Prison

Within the week Louise Gillette found rooms on Hulbert Street in Auburn. Hazel, who had learned of the conviction while in Zion City, followed. For a time Mrs. Gillette attempted to support Hazel and herself by writing, but the big story was fading. The Denver and New York papers had needed Louise only when there was a courtroom drama.[9] Chester was quickly becoming old news and by December seventeenth he had almost disappeared from the front pages.

As 1907 opened the officers in Herkimer County changed roles and George Ward became the new county judge. But the Gillette case was not yet dead in Herkimer. The six doctors who had so annoyed Senator Mills with their "parrot-like" testimony submitted their bills to the county.

The county fathers were flabbergasted. Each physician made a claim for $600. In 1907 this was more than many annual salaries and the board of supervisors rebelled. It approved payment, but for just half—$300 each.[10]

The appeal promised to be expensive. For several weeks Mrs. Gillette attempted to raise funds by lecturing. She appeared in movie theaters in upstate New York and spoke between films. But interest lagged, and by springtime she gave up her lodgings in Auburn and returned to Colorado.[11]

In the Adirondacks where it all started the guides and lumberjacks were slow to forget. The story of the drowning and Chester's travels were told and retold in every camp. Throughout 1907 the woods troubadours carried a new song from one lumber camp to another. No one knew who wrote it and the verses may have had a hundred authors. It was one of those spontaneous ditties that was repeated in the bunk rooms of every lumber camp and in all of the mountain drinking places. As the year went on new verses appeared and no two versions were quite the same. Most dealt with the drowning and Chester's incarceration:

> Away from the sight of the people
>   Where no one could hear her last call,
> Or no one could tell how it happened,
>   But God and Gillette know it all.
>
> He is now in Auburn's dark prison,
>   And soon will give his young life,
> Which might have been full of sunshine
>   Had he taken Grace Brown for his wife.[12]

The verses were endless and by the next winter even school children were singing the ballad of Grace Brown.

Chester was not the only one remembered in verse. A song called "Entreating" quickly appeared in sheet music. The words sounded very familiar to those who had read the Grace Brown letters. They were intended to:

> I'm lonely tonight and I'm thinking of you dear;
> I'm lonely tonight. How I wish you were here.

It was familiar stuff, yet one had to search through the letters to find actual words and phrases which had been coupled together to make the song lyrics. It *sounded* like the real thing, and in case the customer missed the point there was a photo of Grace on the cover.[13] Someone would profit from the tragedy.

As 1906 turned into 1907 Cortland started a fresh leaf and lapsed into its many routines as rapidly as possible. The newspaper had already dropped Chester from the front page and now he disappeared from the inner pages as well. Meanwhile, his former co-workers prepared for the annual Gillette Skirt Company Ball in late January.

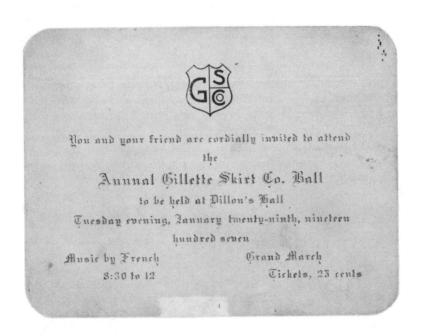

Like the annual picnic the Ball maintained a family image for workers and management alike. For a modest price of twenty five cents each worker and his guest could attend the company function at Dillon's, the local establishment of dance. The Ball was a Tuesday affair, lasting until midnight and ending with a Grand March!

Tuesday certainly was an odd day for a Ball but there was a reason. Horace was preparing to travel. He was taking a vacation from Cortland and the unpleasant memories of the past year. Right after the Ball he and his family took the train to New Orleans and the Mardi Gras. He then placed his wife and son on a ship to Europe.[14] It was time for Horace to return to normal.

Chester's parents were back in Fraser, busy attempting to raise money for the appeal. Their efforts ranged from taking in boarders to working in the sawmill. Louise wrote an unknown young newsman in Central New York State about the family progress. She slowly built up to what she longed for, an offer to write for an upstate paper so that she could be near Chester:

Fraser Colo.
Aug. 26, 1907

My Dear Boy,

You know you always seem like my boy, because of your intense interest, and I shall never forget or fail to appreciate, your love and kindness, and that of your family for one who needed sympathy and help so much.

I was real glad to hear from you once more. I had been wondering why you did not write,—but that wonderful baby was probably taking all your spare time. I shall be so glad to see him and all the rest of the family when I come east again. I cannot say when that will be, but I expect it will not be until spring. It does seem such a long time to wait. I expect to go in to Denver in a few weeks and try to earn something for Chester. I have had two boarders most of the summer, but they go back to school in Sept. One goes east to Princeton college, and the other to Denver University.

Yes, Hazel had written home about why you did not interview her. If I could get on a paper in any capacity in Utica, Syracuse or Auburn I would go east in a few weeks so as to be near Chester and the girls. Lucille begins the study of stenography next week Monday. Hazel will keep on at the mill if she can stand it. It is almost too hard for her. She is tired all the time.

Mr. Gillette and Paul are both working at the mill and getting good pay. We are all bending every energy to raise money to come east. Living is very high here and it is hard to save.

I am real glad you are prospering financially and I wish [sic] you are growing spiritually as well. It does not pay to neglect the spirit while caring for the body. God bless and help you all is my earnest prayer. Why did not your sister answer my letter?

Love to all.

Yours very sincerely,
Louise M. Gillette[15]

Louise M. Gillette, Chester's mother.

The two girls were now both in the East. The younger, Lucille, had chosen to enter a business school in Auburn. Lucille was devoted to her older brother and visited him when it was permitted. She did not come to Auburn unaccompanied. Louise Gillette still had friends in Zion City and persuaded one young woman, Bernice Ferrin, to stay with Lucille while she maintained her vigil in Auburn.

Newsmen who had earlier learned of regular letters from a woman named Lucille had attempted to find scandal in it. Now they discovered the identity of Lucille and her midwestern companion living in the vicinity of the prison. Letters from an admirer were preferable, but a sister was worth at least a few paragraphs.

In the winter of 1907–1908 Mills finally filed his appeal of Chester's conviction. Suddenly the long respite in prison came to a close. Chester was once more in jeopardy. The Appeals Court could save his life or kill him.[16]

January 1908 was the month that the appeal was considered. The case seemed hopeless to most Cortland people but there was one exception. Carrie Gillette, Chester's Aunt Carrie, came from the Pacific Northwest to visit. She was confident that her favorite nephew would be spared.

Carrie's brother, Horace, was equally convinced that Chester would *not* survive the appeal. Uncle Horace took his wife abroad for an extended trip to avoid what he considered to be an impending attempt by the press to reopen old wounds. He would be away until April.[17]

Winter dragged into February before the Court of Appeals announced its decision. By mid-month it was all over. The appeal was denied, and step by step the court demolished Mills' claims that Chester had suffered unfairly at the hands of the Herkimer court:

(1) The evidence *was* circumstantial, but the Appeals Court found that it was convincing nonetheless.

(2) Although Mills had claimed that the extraordinary term of court was unconstitutional, the Appeals Court found that the governor was completely within his rights in granting it.

(3) Mills had objected vigorously about the presence in the courtroom of the fetus in the covered jar. The Appeals Court declared that it was *not* inflammatory, as Mills had charged.

(4) The court upheld the admissibility of Grace's letters.

(5) Mills had charged that the district attorney, in summing up had made erroneous statements not upheld by evidence. The Court

agreed, but pointed out that the defense had objected at the time, that the objections were upheld, and that the jury was instructed accordingly.[18]

It was the end of the line for Chester in New York State Courts, and the death penalty was rescheduled. Execution would occur in the week of March 30th. Chester took the news impassively, though with bitterness, but his family was devastated.[19]

In the days that followed the press played on Chester's stoicism. It made good copy. But Chester now shared the limelight with others. Harry Thaw was still drawing attention, and so was Evelyn Nesbit who promised to divorce him. The public was also following the great New York to Paris auto race. As Chester received the somber news of the appeal the German car was leaving Erie, Pa. and the French car was going through Buffalo.[20]

Louise began to plan one last ditch fight. They came east, Louise, Frank and young Paul. In March they moved to a house in Auburn. Captain Robertson of the Salvation Army generously took the former Army family into his own home on Seminary Street. Frank Gillette was tall, thin, consumptive and exceedingly pessimistic.[21]

Louise still saw a light of hope. Her last stand would be an appeal to the governor. She sent family members far and wide with petitions. She, however, headed for Herkimer county seeking interviews with former jury members. In each case she attempted to see if the juror had doubts about his decision. If he did, it was grist for the little mill she was preparing for the governor.[22]

There was much talk of "new evidence" that Mrs. Gillette was gathering, but little explanation of what it might be. Mills had little to give her—he had exhausted all he thought useful in court. The Gillettes now cited Herkimer stories saying that certain documents, evidence at the trial, had been altered or written in, during the course of the trial.

As the execution date drew closer newspapers began to reexamine the Gillette case. Instead of the occasional color story, journalists began to recapitulate the entire story. It was now over a year since it all began and editors felt that it was necessary to prepare for the impending execution with detailed stories written from the files—stories that covered the whole case from the drowning to the death row watch.

Anything new was worth printing. The challenge to the evidence by Chester's family drew strange letters from people whose memory of the trial was already dimming. One letter asserted that the Grace Brown letters were forgeries, letters taken from a novel called "Confessions of a Wife."[23]

It was an interesting charge, for there was such a novel—it had appeared as a serial in the *Century Magazine* in 1902. Superficially there was a parallel between the novel and the often published letters that had once been used as evidence.

The similarity lay in the fact that the novel was unique in form. It purported to be made up entirely of letters and telegrams from a wife to her husband, family and friends. In it she bared her fears for a foundering marriage. But here the similarity ended, for no three consecutive words of the novel can be found in Grace's missives.[24] Grace's letters were destined to survive longer than any of the people who chose to argue about them in 1908.

Time was running out. By mid-March Mrs. Gillette had gathered her new evidence and gone to Albany. Governor Hughes, freshly installed in his new office, had to confront Louise Gillette. It was an even match—he, chief executive of the Empire State and she, the experienced street warrior, fighting for her son.[25]

There was little really new evidence to show for her door to door campaign but one thing did stand out. Louise presented an allegation that Grace Brown had been epileptic. This somewhat startling announcement promised to serve Chester twice. On the one hand people could now rationalize several ways in which the girl might have fallen out of the boat during a seizure. This was enhanced by the tendency of the public to attribute to epilepsy many things that would be disregarded today.[26]

Chester's supporters hoped to dispute the post mortem findings with this new information. Mrs. Gillette had found a doctor who was willing to testify that many of the characteristics of the body that the examiners had attributed to a death blow could have been the product of epilepsy. Strange as this might sound today, it caused many people to become thoughtful at the time.

The governor was courteous and Mrs. Gillette was properly gracious in describing their meeting. However, he deferred judgment until later. Stories of the day claimed that before the session was over Governor Hughes was on his knees praying with the former street evangelist, and that there were tears in his eyes as they parted.

Hughes did receive the papers Mrs. Gillette left with him, including depositions from several factory workers who claimed that Grace had suffered "spasms" and that it was general knowledge in the factory. Several of the witnesses were called for oral testimony. However one, Ella Hoag, was Chester's cousin and another, Bert Gross, was his friend.[27]

The execution loomed and with only a few days to go Hughes gave his opinion. There was simply too little hard evidence, he felt, to warrant a change in the original verdict.[28] Black, banner headlines announced the decision to the world:

CHESTER GILLETTE MUST DIE

15

DEATH AND AFTERMATH

execution (ek-sē-kū'shon), n. [< ME. execucion (= D. executie = G. execution = Dan. Sw. exekution), < OF. execution = G. execution = Dan. Sw. exekucion = Pg. execução = It. esecuzione = Sp. ejecutio(n-), exsecutio(n-), a carrying out, perform-ance, a prosecution, etc., < exequi, < L. execu-executus, exsecutus, carry out, execute: see exe-cute.] 1. The act or process of completing or accomplishing; the act or process of carrying out in accordance with a plan, a purpose, or an order.

Specifically—5. The carrying out of a death sentence; capital punishment; the act of put-ting to death as directed by a judge of court: as, the execution of a murderer.

Governor Hughes' announcement was a cruel rebuff to the Gillettes. Frank had not really expected the governor to intervene, but Louise entertained hope to the last. Now gloom descended on the little family in Auburn.

They clung to the chance to be near Chester. The week set for execution was but days away and the family divided its time between visiting Chester in the daytime and gathering in the Robertson's house in the evening. Here they huddled by themselves and prayed loudly. Neighbors knew and understood, but the noise could be heard in the street. Captain Robertson moved his family out.[1]

Gillettes were not the only people in the Robertson house. Bernice Ferrin, the friend from Zion City, Illinois stayed to support her friends. Far from being content with merely consoling the family, she made application to the courts to visit Chester. Surprisingly, she was allowed into the prison and permitted to visit Chester in the condemned section. Aside from the clergy she was the only non-relative to gain entry to the prison.[2]

Louise made one last desperate approach to Governor Hughes. It was a question sent by telegram:

Can you say before your God that you have no doubt of Chester's guilt? Please wire. If you cannot then his blood will be upon your head.

(Signed) HIS MOTHER[3]

153

But Governor Hughes, himself a minister's son with prim, upstate roots was adamant. Although such appeals for clemency affected him deeply, he saw no reason to intervene in the judicial process that had originally condemned Chester.

Visits to the prison became part of the daily routine. Now it was the parents who were most likely to visit, but Aunt Carrie came too. Horace was not yet back from Japan.

Chester's contacts with outsiders were becoming more and more limited. He could look forward to his family, but his lawyers were gone. One reporter did threaten a court suit to gain interviews with the prisoner. But unlike Bernice Ferrin he failed to get by the warden's office. Chester was allowed modest contact with other prisoners, reading to some and playing checkers with others.[4]

Apart from his family, he was limited to visits with his spiritual advisors. Cordello Herrick was the official prison chaplain, but in spite of his many months in Auburn, Chester preferred another clergyman.

The Reverend Mr. Henry MacIlravy was from Little Falls and had first visited Chester in the Herkimer jail before the trial. Chester had liked the young minister immediately and a fast friendship developed. Now that the fatal week was approaching he leaned more heavily than ever on the Herkimer County minister who came to Auburn to be close to the condemned man.

Press coverage began to build. The attention devoted to Chester resembled the ballyhoo of the 1906 trial. Now, however, there was little real news to report. Until the actual execution reporters had to work over old history or new tidbits gleaned from the prison staff.

But the staff revealed little, and the press converged on Louise, Frank, Carrie and the young minister. They made good copy but they could tell little about Chester that the press did not already know.

One topic was on everyone's mind—confession. The constant speculation about a confession from Chester suggested that these people believed that confession was good for the soul. The question was, whose soul? Herkimer citizens, in particular, seemed to be concerned. Letters came from complete strangers begging Chester to repent. For a society that believed in capital punishment, this desire for confession appeared to signify uneasiness. What if an error lay buried in the long trial transcript? What if the system had failed?

Suddenly there was no more time. March 29th was the eve of the week set by the court for execution, and it was generally understood that the prison authorities did not wish to drag out the painful duty any longer than necessary.

The prison staff readied the death chamber. The state electrician, E. F. Davis, came to Auburn and tested the cumbersome electric chair. Warden Benham's staff prepared the chamber and set up seats for the required witnesses.[5]

The witnesses, themselves, were in Auburn by the night of the 29th. They included the necessary prison staff, headed by Warden George Benham. From South Otselic came Dr. J. Mott Crumb as a friend of the Brown family. Herkimer county was represented by Henry MacIlravy, the young minister, and A. B. Klock who was now sheriff and who had known Chester since his arrest.[6] Cortland county provided a Charles Mosher, but his link with the Gillette case was a complete mystery.

There were far more requests for admission as a witness than the prison could or would accommodate. Some were turned away for lack of space. Others were obvious thrill seekers. Benham had to contend with two requests that were more difficult. One was from Carrie Nina Gillette—Chester's favorite aunt. The other was from Bernice Ferrin, the Zion City woman who had been so caught up in

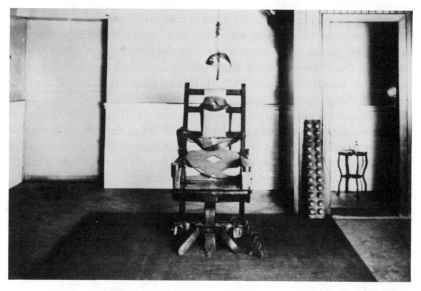

The "Death Chair" at Auburn Prison

Chester's cause. Why these two wished to be present at the execution will never be known. The warden denied both requests.[7]

Syracuse newspapers planned execution editions with tedious summaries of the case. One presented a panorama of the prison, a photograph as wide as the masthead in which the death house was prominently marked. The press was ready.

Before daybreak on March 30th Chester was awakened and given a final opportunity to confer with the minister, Henry MacIlravy. He was quickly led to the tile floored chamber that contained the electric chair. Officials fastened the straps and electrodes.

The signal was given and electrician Davis closed the switch. Chester was jolted by 1800 volts at seven amperes. After one minute he was declared dead. It was just 10:18 a.m.[8]

Several minutes passed while doctors examined the body in the chair. Henry MacIlravy was completely overcome and reeled from the room. But the witnesses, 23 of whom had come from out of town, buzzed until Warden Benham pounded the floor for order. Abruptly it was all over.[9]

Auburn officials were pleased with the execution. It had been quick, clean and merciful—or so it was perceived. It is possible that it might have been just a little more quick and merciful. For one minute they had passed 1800 volts through Chester's body. But the seven amperes of current was low and rather like the current in one's own home. Today's electrical engineers are apt to comment that it is the current, rather than the voltage that poses the greater danger of accidental electrocution. But this was 1908 and the event was anything but accidental.

The execution was proudly described as "The most successful that ever took place in the local prison." That statement brings to mind nineteenth century images of public hangings in Britain and in the American West. It was a grim newspaper that Louise Gillette read that Monday afternoon.[10]

While the press ran off to write those stories, Chester's body was taken to an examining room. Here five physicians performed a perfunctory autopsy. One was Dr. John Gerin who signed the death certificate. Another was Dr. J. Mott Crumb from South Otselic. It was his wife who had been Billy Brown's teacher and friend.[11]

But the leader of the team was Dr. Edward Anthony Spitzka who had come from the Jefferson Medical College in Philadelphia. Spitzka was a specialist in the human brain. Already he had

THE LAST CHAPTER IN A MOST REMARKABLE TRAGEDY.

Chester Gillette in the electric chair in Auburn about to pay the penalty for the brutal murder of the young girl who loved and trusted him.

Typical newspaper sketch of the era.

autopsied several criminals who had been executed and had gained considerable fame only a few years earlier when he led the autopsy on Leon Czolgosz, the man who had assassinated President McKinley.[12]

His interest was borne out in the brief autopsy report. Chester's head measurements were carefully noted. The cranium was opened and the brain removed, measured and set aside. Spitzka signed the autopsy report on behalf of the team.[13]

Now it was the turn of the two men of the cloth. Reporters besieged prison chaplain Cordello Herrick and young Henry MacIlravy from Herkimer County. It was the last gasp of the press in its attempt to find a confession story. The two ministers, after all, were privy to Chester's last conversations. Did he confess? They refused to give a clear answer, but issued a brief joint statement:

> Because our relationships to Chester Gillette was privileged we do not deem it wise to make a detailed statement, and simply wish to say that no legal mistake was made in his electrocution.[14]

Some journalists took this to be an acknowledgement that a

Written the day after the execution by Chaplain of Auburn Prison, this letter seems to indicate a confession by Chester.

deathbed confession had been made to the ministers. Large headlines plastered the word *confession* across more than one newspaper. But it was not quite that clear and the statement can as easily be interpreted that Chester had accepted the "other guilt" theory—that he deserved punishment for the crime of deceiving Grace and abandoning her even if he had not murdered her.

Frank and Louise Gillette went to the Tallman Undertaking Establishment. On Tallman's stationery they wrote out an order to Warden Benham directing that Chester's body be turned over to the undertaker.[15] Some news stories predicted that the Gillettes would take Chester back to Colorado. Others suggested a Cortland cemetery.

But it was neither. Transportation was expensive and the Gillettes were nearly penniless. Next day they buried Chester in a cemetery on the outskirts of Auburn. The grave was unmarked and lay in a row devoted to the interment of lifers, the homeless and unfortunate. His friend, Mr. MacIlravy officiated.[16]

Louise Gillette was satisfied. The wooded cemetery slope would face the warm rising sun each morning. It was a small thing to salvage from the months of grinding bitterness. From the prison officials her husband claimed Chester's last personal possessions— $9.75 in cash, a watch, shirt buttons, studs, cuff buttons and a ring. It was all that was left of Chester.[17] The Gillettes then took their remaining children back to Colorado by way of Zion City.

But not quite all of Chester was buried in the Auburn cemetery. In a moment of bad taste the newspapers cast one last headline about Chester. Dr. Spitzka, the renowned specialist took Chester's brain back to the Jefferson Medical College in Philadelphia. It was all duly reported.[18]

The *Cortland Standard* reported the execution in a front page story, although it avoided the sensational posture adopted by its larger competitors. However, Chester's name did not appear among the list of deaths, births and marriages that day. He was no longer even a vital statistic.

Finally, Central New York returned to normal. Chester's cousin, Harold, went to New York City to meet his father and Mother. Horace had timed it safely. They returned to the United States barely six weeks after the execution. Chester's other cousin, Leslie, now held down the New York City office of the Gillette Skirt Company. Bert Gross and other foremen, including the "detestable Grace Hill" went about their business as usual.

What Central New Yorkers did not yet know was that the Gillette case would never completely go away. It would recur regularly for good reasons and bad for the rest of their lives.

The year 1908 ended quietly at last. During Christmas week Hattie Benedict married a young Cortland lawyer in a private ceremony in the little house on Main Street where Chester had never called.[19]

In the years that followed, Frank Gillette's family disappeared from the Midwest. Horace's children left Cortland one by one and the factory business declined. For four years the country was caught up in the Great War. But by 1923, when Chester would have been forty years old, the press demonstrated that the story would never die.

The *Syracuse Herald*, the paper which had enjoyed the great scoops of 1906, and a paper which should have known better, printed a Sunday feature on the Gillette case. It was not written locally, but was copied from a pulp magazine that specialized in sensational crime. Across the front page of the *Herald* was spread a "fac-simile" of Grace's June 28th letter. The letter was contrived.[20]

At first glance the letter appeared to be a reproduction of Grace's own handwritten letter. This would have been a literary coup since the public had never seen the actual letters used in the trial—only printed reproductions. But a close inspection of the "Facsimile" showed that words were transposed and paragraphs omitted.

It would seem that someone in the editorial offices of the pulp magazine had tossed the Grace Brown letters to a secretary and asked her to copy certain paragraphs in a woman's hand. The meaning of *facsimile* has subtly changed over the years. In the 1980s it implies an exact, even photographic, copy. But in 1923 the word permitted reconstruction as well as reproduction—at least in the newsroom of the *Syracuse Herald*.

Local citizens of Cortland and Herkimer girded themselves to the likelihood that newspapers would run anniversary stories about the Gillette case forever. Except for these, however, most people tended to forget the story as the century wore on. Chester and Grace were gone. Their brothers and sisters married and disappeared into American society. Memories dimmed, and few recalled the sensation of the great trial. The murder case of the century slipped at last into obscurity.

Fac-Simile Fragment of One of Billy Brown's Notes, and Forlorn Girl Whose Life Paid for One Misstep

I am crying and cant half write. Guess its because my sister is playing "Loves Young Dream" on her mandolin and singing it. I am a little blue.

Chester, my silk dress is the prettiest dress I have ever had, or, at least, that is what every one says. Mama dont think I have taken much interest in it. I am frightened every time it is fitted. Mama says she dont see why I should cry everytime they look at me. Chester, dear, I hope you.

had an awfully nice time on the fourth. I dont care, dear, where you go or who you go with if you only come to me on the seventh. I am trying to be awfully brave dear, because I was so glad to hear from you tonight. Do you miss my poor little self at the factory? Dont it seem funny not to have to chase for boxes for me and have me ask for your shears I miss you dreadfully, dear, and I find myself wondering what you are doing and if you miss me. I cant wait till I see you, dear,

(Above) The 1923 "Fac-simile" of Grace's letters that appeared in the *Syracuse Herald.* (Below) Segments of the same letter, taken from the trial manuscript. The hand written version is drawn from widely separated portions of the original. Compare the "Fac-simile" with Grace's own handwriting, page 38.

I am crying and cant [sic] half write. Guess it's because my sister is playing her mandolin and singing 'Love's Young Dream'. I am a little blue. Chester, my silk dress is the prettiest dress I ever had, or at least that's what every one says . . . Chester, dear, I hope you will have an awfully nice time the Fourth. Really, dear, I dont [sic] care where you go or who you go with, if you only come for me on the 7th . . . Do you miss my poor little self in the factory? Dont [sic] it seem funny not to chase for boxes for me and have me ask you for your shears?

16

DREISER'S
GREAT NOVEL

Halfway through the Roaring Twenties the nearly forgotten story of Chester and Grace abruptly returned in a work of fiction. This time the tragic drowning formed the keystone of a best selling novel and the author was America's rising, if controversial, novelist, Theodore Dreiser.

Dreiser's beginnings were humble in the extreme. He was born in Terre Haute, Indiana in 1871 while the Gillette family was raising its young men in Montana.[1] The Dreisers were German Americans with a strong religious cast. The mother was inordinately superstitious and the father was a fervent Catholic whose faith was simple but stifling.[2]

The family struggled along in poverty. There were too many children and not enough money. The Dreisers moved from one town to another and in Terre Haute from one house to another. The father suffered from financial ruin and poor health—an accident had laid him low for many months—and always the family was moving.[3]

As young Dreiser grew he found an occasional, sympathetic teacher who demonstrated an interest in the young man. When he displayed a talent for writing it was encouraged.[4] He drifted into journalism and after leaving the family, went from city to city writing as a staff reporter or special assignment writer, and once in a while he sold an article for magazines. By the 1890s he had made his way to New York City.

Intermittently he crossed paths with his older brother Paul who had more than once disgraced the family and had finally run away. Paul was in turn a seminary dropout, a bad check writer, an actor and a musician. At one time he had made a living playing piano in a bordello. As a songwriter he had changed his name to Dresser and managed a fair degree of success while Theodore was still struggling. Theodore alternated between affection and envy.[5]

A story persists that while in New York City the two brothers collaborated on a song. Dreiser wrote the lyrics for a verse and chorus. Paul provide the melody. Theodore was unimpressed with the result and treated the song as a joke, but "On the Banks of The Wabash" was to become one of America's most famous songs.[6]

Some dusty song books may still bear the names of both Dreiser and Dresser at the top of the music but most historians discount the tale.[7] Still, that one song made Paul Dresser famous in his home state. Dreiser, who became an American celebrity is known and sometimes remembered in Indiana, but it is Paul Dresser who is the state hero.

As the century ended Dreiser started work on his first novel—*Sister Carrie*. It was a different kind of novel. Dreiser parted company with the cautious novelists of the nineteenth century who still dominated the literary scene. He based *Carrie* heavily on his own childhood and youth experiences, describing in great detail the nature of poverty and family troubles. He wrote of common (even coarse) characters. It is a wonder that *Sister Carrie* was ever published.

It barely was. Reviews were lukewarm and sales were low. Not only did the book fail to sell, but Dreiser was accused of writing an immoral book and the publisher temporarily suppressed the work. It was the low point of his life.[8] Once he was reduced to borrowing twenty five dollars on his watch. It was distressing but Dreiser was used to poverty, even if he had dreams of escaping it. At any rate the loan meant new shoes and paid up rent.[9]

As a failed first novelist he turned back to journalism. He surprised his friends by becoming editor of a magazine *The Delineator*.[10] It was a fashion rather than a literary magazine but it was a job. The twentieth century had arrived and Dreiser's luck began to turn. Attitudes slowly changed and *Carrie* began to sell. By 1906 Dreiser could consider himself both an editor and a novelist. It was then that Grace drowned and Chester sat through the ordeal of his trial. Dreiser, like everyone else in the Big City, avidly read the daily accounts of the great trial. He was fascinated.

Like all Americans, Dreiser alternated between the long

164

running story of the Thaw murder case and the plaintive accounts of Grace Brown. The Midwesterner became familiar with the place names of upstate New York, from South Otselic to Herkimer. He never forgot them.

Dreiser continued to write. By 1911 he had produced *Jennie Gerhart* and this time the critics as well as some of the public, were beginning to see Dreiser as a real novelist. It was a bit early to presume that the man from Indiana would become a new Howells or Mark Twain, but he did appear to be a leader. The next fifteen years were filled with novels and autobiographical essays. He even published poetry. Hemingway and Faulkner were emerging but Dreiser, now older, acted as if he had finally arrived. He was well known, if not yet famous, and his book sales gradually improved.

Still, Dreiser was no runaway success and during these fifteen long years he laid plans for his one great work, that blockbuster that every novelist craves. This novel, like *Carrie,* would deal with social themes and lifelike people. Moreover, it would be based on a murder case—a real one. Off and on Dreiser played with the idea, started writing, set it aside and started again.[11]

One problem lay in choosing an actual murder case to fictionalize. Several had caught Dreiser's attention since the turn of the century, and Chester was not the only young man in his clipping file. Still, one theme was consistent. The case must be one in which a man commits murder for the purpose of maintaining or improving his social standing. It also required a love triangle. Such stuff had not been proper raw material for novels in the nineteenth century, but this was a new age.

Not that crime was unknown to the public. Newspapers daily presented an endless list of murder, suicide and terrorism. What Dreiser wished to do was explore the background of the participants and their motives by analyzing each fictional character. Many critics of the day feared that such soul searching would merely dramatize and legitimize the terrible crimes that would be a necessary part of the novel. Dreiser did not.

However, he alternated among various actual cases as he first started, and then tabled the great novel. Finally, in the 1920s he selected the Gillette murder case and began to write in earnest. It was time. An entire generation of readers still remembered the agonizing events of 1906 and the execution of 1908. The cast was ready made. Dreiser needed only to disguise the principals and alter places and events, but only when necessary to achieve the smooth flow of a fictional story.

One might speculate on why Dreiser chose the Gillette case over other murder trials that existed in his files. Many would have provided the plot he needed and most were more gory, more shocking and more salacious but Dreiser identified with the Cortland story.

More specifically, he identified with Chester. The corpulent, successful author from Indiana was very much at home with the story of the young man from Montana, Washington, Ohio, and New York. The yellowing news stories of 1906 painted a picture of poverty, constant moving, a father who was ill, and religion.

Religion, more than anything else struck a familiar note in the mind of the great author. He himself had known a childhood where faith and religious practice had dominated the home. The image of a young Chester following his parents from one street mission to another and living the straight life of Salvation Army families residing in glass houses touched the man.

Chester would become a fictional character with a new name but the story would be seen through his eyes. To Dreiser there was no question of whether it was the Gillette murder case or the Grace Brown murder case or the murder case from Cortland or Herkimer. It was, very simply, the Gillette case. It was Chester's own story.

The novel would begin with the early life of a youth in the Middle West. Fragments of Chester's life were woven together with Dreiser's own memories of growing up in Indiana. After that Dreiser's very fertile imagination expanded the early story until it was truthful to the mood of Chester's own origins yet almost completely fictional in detail.

But when Dreiser progressed to the point of bringing the young man east to an uncle's factory and into a liaison with a young working girl, the thread of the story began to approach the realities of 1906. Dreiser remembered many of the events. Readers of the novel would remember even more and look for them. Dreiser wanted to create an authentic mood and place the story in a familiar Northern New York scene.

Dreiser was in the midst of a liaison of his own. His first marriage had faltered and failed. His wife had left him and lived elsewhere. In the meantime he had begun an affair with Helen Richardson who was both a very distant relation and an aspiring actress. He was to marry Helen later, but at the moment he was truly between marriages.[12]

Helen helped to organize his notes and typed his staggeringly large manuscripts. When Dreiser struck out to find local color for the New York State setting, he invited Helen along on a trip to the famous sites which he had only visited in newspaper clippings. The two started off in a Maxwell car and headed for the North Country.[13]

Travel had changed since 1906. Railroads were giving way to the automobile, but a trip through the Catskills to Central New York in the 1920s was no light undertaking. Roads were muddy and tires self destructed without warning, but Dreiser was adamant. He would visit all the famous places.

The couple "motored" first to Cortland and then to South Otselic to see the Brown farm house. They then drove over the hills to Herkimer and on to the Fulton Chain Lakes. The author made a point of staying at the Glennmore and hired a boat at the very dock from which Chester had set out. He then rowed Helen out over the cold waters of Big Moose Lake. He had found his local color. This time however, the girl came back with the rented boat.[14]

Dreiser's notes helped create the fine detail for place and function that appeared in the second half of the novel. At one time he visited collar factories in Troy which was then the shirt and collar capital of the country. If the fictional factory was to make collars, the fictional workers would have the drudging pace that the Hoosier author noted in the real factory.[15]

Dreiser had no trouble creating an affair between the leading characters of his story. He and Helen worked together on parts of the manuscript. His assistants wallowed through the voluminous manuscript and committed it to typewritten form. The publisher found the novel to be overly long fearing that the two-volume work would intimidate potential buyers. The publisher cut but Dreiser rewrote, stubbornly reinserting lost material.[16]

The final work appeared in bookstores with over 800 pages and cost five dollars. It was late by more than a year and arrived as 1925 turned into 1926. Reviewers were divided, yet the consensus was generally favorable. Dreiser had really written his "big one."

If *The New York Times* reviewer had a mixed opinion it mattered little to Dreiser. The author's portrait dominated the front page of the Sunday Book section. The review found fault with the book's length and with Dreiser's compulsion to create masses of detail. Yet this was Dreiser, and no one imagined that he would approach the novel in any other fashion.

The *Times* review spoke of Dreiser's "Undisciplined power" and treated the book as a "Haunting study of crime and punishment."

Strangely the *Times* reviewer either missed the Gillette connection or chose to ignore it. No mention of Chester, Grace, Cortland or Herkimer crept into the article.[17]

The *New York Herald Tribune* took a very different approach. Its Sunday story contrasted the new novel with the Gillette case and cited clippings from its own and other 1906 newspapers.[18]

In Cortland the novel's release drew only modest attention. The *Cortland Standard* devoted two columns to the *Herald Tribune* story and its allusions to the Gillette case. Among the actual upstate figures however, the *Standard* mentioned only Chester and Grace. No local reporter interviewed living survivors of the trial when the novel appeared.[19]

The Cortland account was buried on an inside page but page one that day featured Evelyn Nesbit. The former wife of Harry Thaw had drunk poison in an apparent suicide attempt following a New Years Eve party.[20] Several days later a photo of the actress appeared in the *Standard*. The onetime showgirl lay in a Chicago hospital receiving treatment.[21]

But no Cortland follow-up story dealt with the new national best seller—and it *was* a best seller. Dreiser would ever after be known as the man who wrote *An American Tragedy*. In Cortland he would be remembered as the man who changed the story.

fact (fakt), *n.* [< L. *factum*, a deed, act, exploit, ML. also state, condition, circumstance (> It. *fatto* = Sp. *hecho* = Pg. *feito* = OF. *fait* (> It. *fet, fet* (> ME. *faite, feit, feet*, E. *fe...fait* ... fact, deed, etc.), neut. of *fa...* ...
2. A real state of th*...*
a statement o*...*
agreeme*...*
a *...*

fiction (fik'shon), *n.* [= F. *fiction* = Pr. *ficxio*, *fiction* = Sp. *ficcion* = Pg. *ficção* = It. *fizione*, *finzione*, < L. *fictio(n-)*, a making, fashioning, a feigning, a rhetorical or legal fiction, < *fingere*, pp. *fictus*, form, mold, shape, devise, feign: see *feign*.] 1. The act of making or fashioning. [Rare.]
2. The act of feigning, inventing, or imagining; a false deduction or conclusion: as, to be misled by a mere *fiction* of the brain.
3. That which is feigned, invented, or imagined; a feigned story; an account which is a product of mere imagination; a false statement.
4. In *literature*: (*a*) A prose work (not dramatic) of the imagination in narrative form; a story; a novel.

17

DREISER—
FACT AND
FICTION

The Chester Gillette/Grace Brown lovers' quandary forms the nucleus of Theodore Dreiser's *An American Tragedy*. The novel adapts, but takes liberties with, original documentation. Dreiser utilized newspaper accounts of the case for background information and visited all of the principal points of interest to gain an insight into the personalities of Gillette and Brown.

On first inspection, Dreiser made no changes in so far as the facts of the case are concerned. He deviated only slightly from exact measurements, numbers, names and degree of emotion. The author was a newspaperman, after all, and thus a fanatic for detail. He adhered so closely to the truth that in the final scenes, he merely paraphrased parts of the actual courtroom testimony.

Opponents and proponents have reflected on the quality of Dreiser's literary genius or lack of it. On one hand it was natural for newsman Dreiser to use newspaper articles as a suggestive outline. He was comfortable with this particular form of source material. His early days in Chicago and St. Louis were preoccupied with a keen awareness of wealth as a means to success. Even as a youth Dreiser had been overwhelmed by magazine stories in which a young woman married and achieved material success. While there were several sensitive and highly publicized murders with which Dreiser would have been familiar, he chose the death of Grace Brown as the platform on which to stage *An American Tragedy*.

One can argue for either unconscious plagiarism or literary genius on the part of Dreiser. The following comparisons are offered as a curious exploration of fact and fiction. They also serve as an enquiry into the possibilities open to Dreiser for sheer brilliance.

Researchers, critics and writers have all taken opposing sides in the arguments regarding Dreiser's novel. There are learned theses proving the validity of Dreiser's greatness in American literature. There is an equal number of arguments showing unequivocally the sham that *An American Tragedy* is. If, indeed, this is a mere flash of literary genius, then Dreiser has still managed to maintain his right to be called brilliant. He wrote simply (if voluminously) and with an insight which peaked the reader's curiosity. He touched on such a wide range of topics as to lend credence to both sides of the argument. For there is another side. Dreiser was a borrower, and in borrowing he forced his reader to separate his genius from that of history.

The preceding chapters have set forth the story as it actually occurred. Dreiser added to this with imagination. It is helpful for the reader to attempt to discriminate between the two.

It is instructive to compare the original newspaper accounts with Dreiser's final (and fictional) product.[1] On first inspection Dreiser appears to have made only minor alterations in the Gillette case as he moved it away from the realm of fact. Then obvious changes become apparent, for names of people have been substituted throughout.

Of all the characters in the story, Chester seems to suffer least. He retains his initials as he becomes Clyde Griffiths. "Billy" Brown is reincarnated as "Bobby" Alden. There are no initials here but the retention of a boyish nickname left no doubt in readers' minds as to the parallel identity of the young girl.

When the reader gives close scrutiny to the text of the novel, even more glaring differences emerge. Dreiser, after all, had to avoid naming the villages and cities where actual characters of the story lived. As a result, Cortland disappears and in its literary (but not geographic) place is Lycurgus. The site of the industrial city was carefully removed to another part of New York State, and although they tried, Cortland people could not actually claim to find themselves and familiar places in the novel.

Similarly, the trial site, the death lake, and the nearby chain of mountain lakes all appear somewhat out of geographic proportion and with new, but vaguely familiar names. Only Utica survived the plowshare as Dreiser turned over one set of characters and sites only to create another, some of which were close images of the first. Like a modern screenwriter who creates a motion picture script from an earlier novel, Dreiser carefully sculptured a novel out of an earlier event, the Gillette case. There would be differences, some for legal reasons and some to meet the needs of fiction.

If people in Cortland and Herkimer were unable to find themselves in fiction it rarely stopped them from thinking that they had. To this day it is an agonizing experience for the person who knows the Gillette case to read the novel without mixing real and fictional names to the point of frustration. Ideally he should start with a list of matching names. Some parallels are close while others are distant and tenuous. Nonetheless, the reader should inspect them:

FACT	FICTION
Chester Gillette	Clyde Griffiths
Frank S. Gillette (Chester's father)	Asa Griffiths (Clyde's father)
Louise M. Gillette (Chester's mother)	Elvira Griffiths (Clyde's mother)
Noah H. Gillette (Chester's uncle)	Samuel Griffiths (Clyde's uncle)
Harold Gillette (Chester's cousin)	Gilbert Griffiths (Clyde's cousin)
Grace "Billy" Brown	Roberta "Bobbie" Alden
Frank B. Brown (Grace's father)	Titus Alden (Roberta's father)
Minerva Brown (Grace's mother)	Mrs. Alden (Roberta's mother)
Pauline (Grace's sisters) Frances Hazel Ruby Mary	Emily (Bobbie's sister)
Carl Clayton (Grace's bothers)	Gifford Tom (Bobbie's brothers)
Ada Hawley (Grace's married sister)	Agnes Gabel (Bobbie's married sister)
Clarence Hawley (Grace's brother-in-law)	Fred Gabel (Bobbie's brother-in-law)

FACT	FICTION
Mrs. Carrie Wheeler (Grace's landlady)	Mrs. Gilpin (Roberta's landlady)
Olive Wheeler (landlady's daughter)	Stella Gilpin (landlady's daughter) ·
George W. Ward (district attorney)	Orville W. Mason (district attorney)
Isaac Coffin (coroner)	Fred Heit (coroner)
Charles D. Thomas Senator A. M. Mills (defense attorneys)	Reuben Jephson Alvin Belknap (defense attorneys)
Irving R. Devendorf (presiding judge)	Frederick Oberwaltzer (presiding judge)
James H. Higby (JP) (arraigned Chester)	Gabriel Gregg (JP) (arraigned Clyde)
Austin B. Klock (undersheriff)	Nicholas Kraut (deputy sheriff)
Mrs. Lizzie Crane (Chester's landlady)	Mrs. Peyton (Clyde's landlady)
Harriet Benedict (a lawyer's daughter)	*
*	Sondra Finchley (Society girl)
Roy Higby (found Grace's body)	John Pole (found Bobbie's body)
Edward Rockwell (Grace used his phone to to call Chester)	C. B. Wilcox (Bobbie used his phone to call Clyde)
Fred S. Gardner (Postmaster, South Otselic)	Roger Beane (Postmaster, Biltz)
Earl Crego (Guide)	Thomas Barrett

---

*Sondra Finchley was a creation of Dreiser's imagination. He attempted to carry on where George Ward had left off in the creation of a love triangle. Many readers, however, took for granted that the two were the same.

FACT	FICTION
Morrell E. Tallett (station agent, DeRuyter)	John Troescher (station agent, Fonda)
Charles A. Doody (desk clerk, Utica)	Frank W. Schaefer (desk clerk, Utica)
William Martin (proprietor, Hotel)	Jerry K. Kernocian (general manager Renfrew House, Utica)
Clara Greenwood (waitress, Tupper Lake)	Blanch Pettingill (waitress, Grass Lake)
Silas Feeter (surveyor)	Rufus Forster (surveyor)
Mrs. P. J. Carey (cottager who heard a scream)	Mrs. Rutger Donahue (cottager who heard a scream)
Holridge & Getman (Undertakers, Frankfort, N.Y.)	Lutz Brothers (Undertakers, Bridgeburg. N.Y.)
Robert Morrison (boat livery)	Sim Shoop (guide and boat livery)
Gladys Westcott Josephine Patrick (Girls Chester met on Adirondack trip)	Violet Taylor Wynette Phant (Girls Clyde met on Adirondack trip)
Theresa Dillon (Grace's friend in Cortland)	Grace Marr (Roberta's friend in Lycurgus)
G. H. Smith Little Falls, N.Y.	Dr. Mitchell Bridgeburg, N.Y.
A. O. Douglas Little Falls, N.Y.	Dr. Betts Bridgeburg, N.Y.
W. E. Hayes Frankfort, N.Y.	Dr. Bavo Coldwater, N.Y.
S. S. Richards Frankfort, N.Y.	Dr. Lincoln Coldwater, N.Y.
J. M. Crumb South Otselic, N.Y.	Dr. Webster Utica, N.Y.
E. H. Douglas Little Falls, N.Y.	Dr. Beemis Utica, N.Y.

FACT	FICTION
	Dr. Sprull Albany,N.Y.
(The medical team which performed an autopsy on Grace)	(The medical team which performed an autopsy on Roberta)
Henry MacIlravy (Spiritual advisor to Chester)	Duncan McMillan (spiritual advisor to Clyde)
Charles Evans Hughes (governor of New York)	David Waltham (governor of New York)
Robert H. Fuller (secretary to the governor)	Robert Fessler (secretary to the governor)

In spite of changes in names and places, Dreiser's reliance on the original Gillette case is strikingly evident. Only in the early pages where he developed the childhood of Clyde Griffiths was he working more with imagination than fact. And small wonder, for in the trial records and news stories which Dreiser digested, Chester's early life was passed over quickly. Only his missionary origins were well known and this Dreiser also wove into Clyde's early life.

It is after the fictional Clyde Griffiths has an affair with a working girl and falls in love with a wealthy debutante that Dreiser began to mine his hoard of resource material. At this point the novelist began to follow fact closely, but not exactly. It is the trip to the Adirondacks that first stirs memories of the Gillette story.

On July 9th, Chester Gillette arrived in Utica with Grace Brown. He registered in a hotel as Mr. and Mrs. Charles George. In fiction, Clyde and Roberta arrive in Utica on July 6th and register as Mr. and Mrs. Charles Gordon.

Next day Chester took his companion by railroad to Tupper Lake. Clyde and Roberta leave Utica for the fictional town of Grass Lake. In each case the town is strange and the real Chester was as uncomfortable in the mountain community as his fictional counterpart is.

By Wednesday Chester and Grace entered the Glennmore at Big Moose Lake, where Chester used the name Carl Grahm. Clyde Griffiths arrives at Big Bittern Lake on a Thursday and identifies himself as Clifford Golden. By now the reader is surrounded by the initials "C. G."

The real Chester took his suitcase and tennis racket with him while Grace left a hat on the hotel rack. The fictional character takes to the boat a bag and tripod while his companion leaves her hat and coat at the inn.

At Big Moose the boat was found near the shore of South Bay with a man's hat and a girl's coat. Grace's body was in eight feet of water about 250 feet from shore. Her body showed bruises and abrasions. In fiction the boat is found along the south shore of the lake with a man's hat. The girl's body lies in about eighteen feet of water about 500 feet from shore.

Chester swam to shore, changed into dry clothes and packed his wet garments into the suitcase. He threw away his umbrella and buried the tennis racket under a log. Dreiser's young man swims ashore, recovers his bag, changes clothes and packs away the wet ones. He buries the tripod under a log.

Gillette walked south, passed three men along the trail and continued to Eagle Bay. Here he took a steamboat across the lake to the Arrowhead Hotel. Griffiths goes into the woods, walks south, meets three people on the trail and walks on to Three Mile Bay. Here he boards a steamboat for Sharon.

Chester was arrested on Saturday July 14th at the Arrowhead Hotel by District Attorney Ward and Undersheriff Klock. Clyde is arrested on Monday July 12th at Shelter Beach by District Attorney Mason and Deputy Sheriff Nicholas Kraut. Were it not for the fictional names of people and places the story might have been a description of fact.

Ward sought and obtained a special term of court rather than wait until the next year. The fictional Mason also obtains a special term of the supreme court. In each case the trial commenced in the autumn months following the summer tragedy.

It took five days for the real jury to be selected and it consisted of farmers, a mail carrier a blacksmith and a mechanic. In fiction, too, it requires five days of jury selection. The final panel contains farmers, storekeepers, a salesman and an insurance agent. It is here that one of the more subtle distinctions between fact and fiction becomes apparent. This was to be no period piece. Dreiser wrote *Tragedy* as a contemporary story. Salesmen and insurance agents were much more common in the 1920s than in Gillette's time.

In Herkimer Mr. Brown, as a witness described Grace's home life, her nickname "Billy" and her June vacation during which she had clothes made. A fictional witness, Titus Alden tells of his daughter Roberta, or "Bobbie," and how she came home to make new clothes.

The details of the fatal trip are pieced together by Dreiser's

175

district attorney who uses many witnesses who were co-workers, fellow passengers on the train and one Blanche Pettingill. She testifies that she is a waitress at the Grass Lake House where the couple had dinner and that they had argued during the meal. It is all too much like the testimony of Clara Greenwood, the waitress from Tupper Lake.

Five doctors testified for the prosecution in Herkimer. They had been among those who conducted the autopsy and they stated that the girl's death was directly or indirectly a result of a blow to the head. The seven fictional doctors considered the case of Roberta Alden. They find that Roberta was alive, though possibly unconscious when she entered the water.

In one respect Dreiser was compelled to deviate from the original. Despite Ward's attempts in Herkimer to make a full-blown affair out of Chester's acquaintance with Harriet Benedict such a romance was doubtful at best. But Dreiser was not restrained by actual events. He developed a new character in the form of a beautiful and wealthy young woman, Sondra Finchley to catch the eye of young Clyde Griffiths. One might wish that Dreiser had created Sondra beautiful and left it at that. The baby talk which emanates from this character is scarcely believable.

The fictional Finchley family is so powerful that at the trial Sondra is never called as a witness. Indeed, her name is never uttered. Rather, she is mentioned in Dreiser's trial only as "Miss X." In real life the New York State courts were not as easily corrupted. Harriet Benedict was mentioned often at the trial and suffered the pressures of giving testimony as well.

In both truth and fiction, the accused takes the stand in his own defense. In each case the prosecution cross examines with vigor. In each case it brings out some of the young man's early background. And in each case the story about the ride on the lake becomes contradictory and dubious.

As the trials, real and imaginary, grind to an end each judge charges his jury. Judge Devendorf, in Herkimer, said: "If the jury finds that Grace Brown jumped overboard voluntarily, and that the defendant made no attempt to rescue her, that does not make him guilty, and the jury must find the defendant *not guilty*."[2]

Dreiser spent little effort on *his* judge's address to the jury. Judge Oberwaltzer says: "If the jury finds that Roberta Alden accidentally or involuntarily fell out of the boat and that the defendant made no attempt to rescue her, that does not make the defendant guilty and the jury must find the defendant *not guilty*."[3]

176

After Dreiser's jury foreman, Lund, announces a verdict of "guilty in the first degree" Clyde telegraphs his family the words: "Mother—I am convicted." Dreiser was making sure that the mother was a prominent figure in the condemned man's family. In life this was true too, but Chester Gillette, upon receiving his sentence had wired an identical message to his *father.*

Like Louise Gillette, Mrs. Asa Griffiths comes east to be with her son during the sentencing. Like Louise she is a temporary reporter for a Denver newspaper. As in life, she follows her son to the prison town of Auburn and lectures to raise money.

Dreiser made use of a legal appeal which, of course, is unsuccessful. Clyde leans upon a minister who has befriended him. One sees here the ghost of the Reverend Henry MacIlravy who follows the real Chester to the death chamber. For reasons best known to himself, Dreiser moved the execution ahead by two hours.

During the course of the trial in Herkimer the greatest public interest lay in the famous letters that Grace had sent to Chester prior to the Adirondack journey. Dreiser was quite aware of the impact of these documents and cleverly wove into *An American Tragedy* portions of Roberta's letters to Clyde. Not surprisingly, they closely resemble Grace's own letters. Where Grace often referred to "blue" moods, Roberta also used the phrase. A typical letter ended with the simple statement "I am blue."

Among the thousands of words in Dreiser's novel, few seem to have been written in error. It is a tribute to his assistants and to his publisher's copy readers. One slip did occur and it came when Dreiser borrowed heavily from Grace's last letter—the one in which she said goodby to her favorite places. The words are extremely close to Grace's own:

> I have been bidding good-by to some places to-day. There are so many nooks, dear, and all of them so dear to me. . . First there was the springhouse with its great masses of green moss. . .Then the 'believe' a cute little house in the orchard. . .[4]

It was the *believe* over which Dreiser or his copy readers tripped. Most of the paragraph was lifted bodily from Grace's last letter which spoke of a *beehive* in the orchard. (See page 73)

Most readers slip by this line without questioning the strange presence of a verb form used as a noun. Translators, however, have found the word to be a stumbling block. Dreiser had intended that the novel should be a social document and in the Soviet Union it was warmly received as an indictment of the American social system. Soviet translators encountered the "believe" line and rendered the word into Russian as a form of "belief."

The German translator attempted to replace it with a colloquial phrase to which his readers could relate. In the German edition the word "believe" is rendered as "Ewig dein" which roughly translates as "forever yours." It has been said that the phrase has been carved on half the tree trunks of Germany, and perhaps this is what the translator saw in Roberta Alden's orchard.

Perhaps the greatest discrepancy occurs when the reader attempts to debate the central character's guilt or innocence. Dreiser portrayed the controversial figure as a man who could not be held responsible for his actions. Most of Dreiser's friends, and more than a few of his detractors, felt that the author saw himself in the form of Clyde Griffiths.

Dreiser's background, not surprisingly, parallels Chester Gillette's own history. It was only natural for Dreiser to capitalize on what he knew best—himself. Dreiser, too, grew up in poverty, always yearning to rise up above what he saw around him. Dreiser was unsuccessful with the women in his life, a fact which helped him to empathize with Gillette. Without being as outwardly enthusiastic as Chester, Dreiser longed for financial independence long after he had achieved it. He was a man who had a talent for writing and after a long, slow start finally made use of the reality that America had thus far ignored. He was a realist. It was for this that most of the criticism of his novel stemmed.

The one great pitfall introduced by the novel is the tendency (almost a compulsion) to pass judgment on Chester and Grace after reading about the fictional Clyde and Roberta. Even more damage may be done by judging other characters of the Gillette saga through the actions of Dreiser's fictional counterparts.

The novelist, after all, writes not only dialog, but gives his readers the very thoughts of his characters. Little wonder that the novel has brought forth mystery, pleasure, suspense, and to the historian, utter confusion.

Miss "X" Miss "X" Miss "X" Miss "X" Miss "X" Miss "X" Miss "X" Miss "X" Miss "X"

18

MOVIES AND MYTHS

Theodore Dreiser's monumental novel was only the beginning, for the fictionalization of the Gillette Story was destined to go on and on. At least two stage versions of *An American Tragedy* appeared. The first was that of Patrick Kearney, chosen by Dreiser as the one who would maintain the theme of realism on stage. There is little in the way of review—critical or otherwise—regarding Kearney's stage attempt which was produced in 1926.

Possibly because he had married an actress, Dreiser was quite partial to dramatic versions of the story. On a visit to the USSR Dreiser was pleased at the popular reception his novel was given as a translation of American literature. He was puzzled, however, that the Soviets were not producing the play. The answer finally came out. The dramatic version presented a factory setting in which the employer-employee relationship was much too informal, if not familiar, to match the Soviet image of capitalist America.[1]

But Broadway touched only a few of the American millions. By the thirties the depression-bound country had found retreat in the great silver screen. Talkies had just replaced the silent movie and the country thirsted for dramatic movies. *An American Tragedy* was among the first of the new breed.

The screen rights of *An American Tragedy* were sold to Paramount Pictures. It was a stormy settlement involving Dreiser, Horace Liveright and Jesse Lasky of Paramount Famous Players. The center of the controversy revolved around a commission to Liveright who was Dreiser's publisher. Liveright was to receive ten

179

percent of the motion picture rights if *Tragedy* was ever sold. A subsequent agreement was reached in which Liveright would receive ten per cent up to $30,000 but no commission on anything over that figure. Dreiser told Liveright the asking price for the movie would be $100,000 from Paramount. Liveright wanted everything over $60,000 if Dreiser managed to get that price. Ultimately Dreiser received $90,000 and Liveright claimed all over $60,000. Dreiser told him he would get his ten per cent and no more.[2]

The film appeared in 1931 produced by the renamed Paramount Publix Corporation under the direction of the great film pioneer, Josef von Sternberg. There had been trouble between von Sternberg and Dreiser from the very beginning. After so many personality clashes it is little wonder the film followed the novel by more than four years!

The motion picture retained the name of the novel and repeated most of Dreiser's now-familiar characters. It was a straightforward treatment of the novel, photographed in black and white with a shrill, though forceful, dialogue. Moviegoers were treated to several stars of the day.[3]

Clyde Griffiths, the young man so carefully patterned on Chester Gillette was played by Phillips Holmes, while Sylvia Sidney was the little factory worker who died in the lake. Sternberg cast Frances Dee as the rich young woman to capture Clyde's heart. Irving Pichel excelled as the formidable district attorney.

In October of 1931 a special screening of the film was attended by Dreiser. The author took legal action to stop the film from being shown to the public. He was outraged and claimed that the movie completely misrepresented the novel. Supreme Court Justice Gragam Witschief of White Plains N.Y. ruled that the film was a faithful representation of the book.

Many reviewers suspected that the action was an attempt to garner publicity for the film. If so it helped very little for reviews were lukewarm. Except for the courtroom scenes the picture was simply too harsh.[4]

But this was not the only lawsuit. As the movie opened in smaller theaters across the country millions of middle aged Americans looked forward to seeing for the first time what they perceived to be a movie version of familiar 1906 events. In Norwich, N. Y. near the little town from which Grace Brown had come, the local theater reportedly advertised with old news stories about Chester and Grace. Mrs. Brown, Grace's mother, promptly sued the theater and Paramount studios as well. The suits dragged on, and with changes of venue, the legal procedures threatened to outlive Mrs. Brown, herself. An out of court settlement finally ended the affair with Paramount.[5]

In 1951, a generation later, and two generations after the Gillette trial, Paramount remade the story. This version was titled *A Place in the Sun* and was directed by George Stevens. The script was substantially updated and moved the story from New York State to the California Sierras. Most of the exterior scenes were shot in the area around Lake Tahoe.[6]

The new script, like the novel and movie which preceded it, made the story a contemporary one, with all of the automobiles and technology of mid-century America. Stevens chose, however, to retain the black and white medium, even in the glittering California mountains. The harsh shadows of black and white photography lent credence to the awful events that took place on the surface of the lake.

For some unexplained reason the new screenwriters changed the names of all the characters. The young man who deserted a pregnant factory girl for a rich debutante became George Eastman. The trail back through Clyde Griffiths to the real Chester Gillette is long and obscure.

Stevens had at his disposal some of the best of Hollywood's screen actors. Young George Eastman (working in his uncle's swim suit factory) was played by Montgomery Clift. Opposite him Stevens cast Elizabeth Taylor as the rich girl and Shelly Winters as the factory worker. With Raymond Burr as the glowering district attorney, it was a stalwart cast, but it was fiction—all fiction—and in its way it would add to the folklore that had already begun to grow up about the life and death of Chester Gillette.

The folklore that has evolved is a combined product of the facts of the Gillette case as remembered by the older generation, and the various changes and additions offered by Dreiser and screenwriters. No small part of the folklore sprang from errors in recalling each. The stories which persist today range from near truth to outright myth.

Cortland residents know that theirs is the factory town of 1906. In other parts of New York State the location of the "real" town is more obscure. A recurring story is the claim that the actual factory was located in Troy on the Hudson River. Unlikely as this might appear it has a basis in the novel. The Griffith company made collars, if only fictional ones. Troy had once been known as the shirt and collar capital of New York State. Dreiser's visit to Troy continues to pay strange dividends and it is all too easy to jump from the fictional product to an actual city.

At one time or another New Yorkers are apt to hear that the real factory town was Auburn, or Utica, or Herkimer. The only thing that these towns have in common with each other and with the Gillette case is that each was named in the Gillette publicity, although never as a factory town.

Perhaps the most frequently misquoted "fact" about the Gillette story is the lake on which the fatal boat ride was taken. In the area around Cortland casual remarks locate the ride on Little York Lake or even on Skaneateles Lake. Each is understandable. In the massive testimony of the trial both lakes are mentioned—as vacation places prior to Chester's last trip.

One might expect that others would remember the death lake more accurately, but Big Moose, for some reason, escapes the mind all too quickly. Visitors to the state are apt to be sent to Raquette Lake, Fourth Lake, and even Tupper Lake as the "Place where it happened." Again, each place was mentioned and mentioned frequently in the trial testimony.

"Facts" based on truth and then distorted into fiction have often returned to the newspapers as truth. On anniversary dates of the drowning or the murder trial generations of cub reporters have been sent to the files, each to write a feature story that would strike a chord in the memory of old timers. Every ten years such features have shortened the story, compressed the time frame and re-introduced old myths.

One early example was a story written by Inez Wallace in the Cleveland *Plain Dealer*. She had the advantage of writing from experience, claiming to have been a young girl who had come to the Glennmore to pick up the mail just as Chester and Grace began their boat ride.[7]

Her account is reasonably accurate, though emotional. In establishing Chester's background she represented the Gillette Company as a *shirt* factory. This was to become one of the most common mistakes in the many newspaper recapitulations.

In 1950 the Syracuse *Post Standard* treated a story about the transfer of title of the Glennmore Hotel. The current facts may well have been true but the historical recap left much to be desired. Here Chester and Grace were given two or three days at the Glennmore prior to the fatal boat ride. To add insult to injury the execution was moved up one month to February.[8]

For many years *The American Weekly* was a popular magazine

section for Sunday newspapers. In a long article about the Gillette Case, Lewis Thompson rode rampant across the facts of 1906. This account started with the arrival of Carl Graham at the Glennmore. The actual register entry Chester made at Big Moose was spelled *Grahm* but nearly half of subsequent accounts misspell the name.

Thompson took his readers through a long drawn out search for Chester led by undersheriff Klock. In this tale Klock traced the trail of Chester and Grace through South Otselic and Cortland before encountering Bert Gross in Cortland and discovering from him the fact that Chester was in the Adirondacks.[9]

Klock's buggy ride through Central New York was as impossible as it was unlikely and may have stemmed from bad memories and misunderstood interviews. Klock, of course, had traveled directly to the Adirondacks with the district attorney. Thompson made no mistake on the date of execution but, unfortunately, moved it to Sing Sing in downstate New York.

In 1963 the Syracuse *Herald Journal* whose dusty files contain some of the original Gillette stories, compounded the misinformation about the case in an AP story from Inlet. Here, in an account of the Arrowhead hotel site, Chester and Grace were pictured as staying at the hotel on the last night of Grace's life. Grace never saw the Arrowhead, and had never been to Inlet. It was Chester who stayed here—after the drowning.[10]

The Inlet reporter innocently passed on two other bits of common error. Chester was pictured as a young man who had spent two years at Oberlin College. It was a reasonable mistake—most people confused the college with the preparatory school, even at the time. But this writer, too, erred in the nature of the Cortland factory. Again it was represented as a shirt factory. One might recall that N. H. Gillette owned a factory that made skirts and shirtwaists, a woman's garment, but never men's shirts.

Not every newspaper review has been couched in error, nor are the errors always serious. One of the best stories appeared sixty years after the event. Readers in St. John's, Newfoundland could find in a Ruth Reynolds story an excellent recap and a factually truthful one. Reynolds stumbled in only two areas. Like many others she used the "Graham" spelling, and she attributed to Chester the idea of taking the boat ride on the lake. Few people note in the trial testimony that Chester's first wish was a steamboat ride on the lake![11]

Still, the trend continues. In 1967 Frank J. Early, an old

newsroom man from Syracuse summarized many of Edith Cornwall's achievements at the Gillette trial. Unfortunately, in doing so he repeated one of Miss Cornwall's graver errors. While interviewing the Brown's in 1906 that lady noted that the youngest daughter was Ruby. Straying somewhat from the truth, possibly for impact, she invented the names of Emerald, Garnet, Opal and Pearl for Grace's other sisters. It was an old mistake but Early cast it in print again and today rumors still circulate in Central New York to the effect that all the Brown girls were named for jewels.[12]

During the great trial in Herkimer the public had been entranced by the introduction as evidence of the boat, the tennis racket, the camera and of course, the letters. The use of these items in fictional versions of the story only confirmed in the minds of the public the images they had formed earlier.

In fact, however, most of the evidence disappeared in the months and years after the trial. Researchers who were prompted by Dreiser's story could find none of these prize items by the 1920s. They had vanished.

In the past half century there has been an overabundance of stories which attempt to account for the loss. No doubt the items were all held by Herkimer County until after the last appeal and execution. Then they quietly slipped away. It is probable that most of them were appropriated by county officers as souvenirs. Today the families which possess the materials either fail to recognize their importance or are embarrassed to admit their existence.

To account for the disappearance, the public has provided its own accounts. Herkimer abounds in stories of the lost boat. According to some it was sold. Others claim it was stolen. A perennial tale in Herkimer describes how a renovation crew, upon removing a masonry wall in the courthouse, came upon the dusty boat, which had been hidden from view for years. Unfortunately, it promptly disappeared again. Others claim to have seen it in the Adirondacks, sunk to the gunwales in mud.

The smaller exhibits provide their own stories. It is reasonable to assume that like the Brooklyn Bridge, Chester's camera or the letters of Grace Brown could be sold on the streets of Herkimer many times over in the course of a year. Sadly, they are often discussed but rarely seen.

One wonders how myths from the Dreiser years could persist into the 1980s. Unfortunately, the most irritating fault of myth and folklore is that they give falsehood a robust and lasting constitution.

Misinformation about the Gillette case continues to abound and it often has it roots in Dreiser.

As recently as 1974 a factual account of the Gillette case appeared in print. The author was none other than a much honored and respected elder of the Adirondacks, Roy C. Higby. Higby was, in fact, the young boy who had ridden the steamboat on the search for Grace Brown and had been the one to see the body in the dark waters of South Bay.

Higby had told and retold the story of the search for decades to fascinated visitors to his retreat on Big Moose Lake. He was prevailed upon to write down his rich memoirs of Adirondack life and publish them. No one was ever more qualified.[13]

Still, in the chapter that deals with the tragic death of Grace Brown, something fails. There is no problem with the events related to the search. Higby was there and his recall is dependable. The problem lies in the rest of the chapter. When Higby came to describe who Chester and Grace were, and how they happened to be at Big Moose he drew not from newspaper files, but from memory. Unfortunately, his memory tended to be influenced by the details of *An American Tragedy*.

In Higby's account Chester Gillett [*sic*] comes from Kansas City. Chester is represented as Grace's foreman. Chester registers at the Glennmore as Carl Graham and after the death Chester proceeds to Inlet where he joins friends and even his rich girlfriend. At the trial, Chester is defended by a lawyer employed by his uncle. During the trial, the other girl, from a fine family, was referred to as "Miss X."

Most of these slips in fact are drawn directly from Dreiser. Yet none detracts from the very important role of Roy Higby. He is an Adirondack guide and resort owner, not an historian. The Gillette background he has related is what most people today think that they remember. And they do, but what they remember is the novel and the movies, not fact.

Each year new myths appear, but the most commonplace are:

That Chester was illegitimate. (He was not.)
That Chester came from Kansas City.
That the factory was the largest in Cortland. (It was quite modest in size.)
That the factory made collars.
That the factory made shirts.
That the factory made razor blades.

185

That Chester had a university education. (He attended Oberlin's preparatory school.)

That Chester was no older than Grace.

That Chester rose to the rank of foreman.

That Grace was tall and slender. (She was certainly slender, but at five feet she was far from tall.)

That the Brown farm was small.

That the trial was held in Cortland.

That Chester met and had extensive social contact with the two normal school girls at Inlet.

That Grace died under a full Moon. (The moon was waning and approaching the third quarter.)

That Chester was executed at Sing Sing.

That Chester and Harriet were engaged.

That Chester made a formal confession.

As the years pass the list will likely become longer.

19

WHATEVER BECAME OF . . .?

Eighty years have passed since Grace Brown died in Big Moose Lake. Few things remain unchanged in eight decades and the Gillette Case is no exception. Only one or two participants are still alive and many have disappeared altogether. Both places and institutions have undergone immense change.

THE PLACES

Cortland remains a small city and county seat. The two rail stations stand next to seldom-used tracks and are no longer active depots. Today Cortland lies directly on Interstate 81, and visitors enter the community by bus and automobile.

The normal school has undergone extensive change. In 1919 a disastrous fire burned down the one building which Chester had known in 1906. The school relocated on what was then the edge of the city where it later grew into a State University College. Today the campus sprawls across two miles of land and its five thousand bluejeaned students come from across New York State and around the world.

Most of the original houses still stand. The one exception is that of N. H. Gillette whose graceful home on West Court Street was razed in 1956 to make way for a small, one-story commercial building. Today the Niagara Mohawk Power Company uses it as a city office.

The little house in which Grace first lived with her married sister is the home of a Cortland fireman. The parlor in which Grace

The Hotel Glennmore, circa 1924, after being remodeled.

first entertained Chester is a warm, modern living room which has recently seen graduation parties and wedding receptions.

The Wheeler house where Grace later roomed now shelters a veterinary service. Chester's last rooming house in East Main Street also remains, as do his other rooming and boarding houses in the same block. A short distance away Hattie Benedict's home seems small but a bit of 1906 remains. A little white gazebo stands among the trees in the shaded yard.

The boxlike factory building remains between Homer Avenue and Miller Street like a grim reminder of the past. Its concrete blocks are now painted red and every window is covered. It serves as a retail furniture and appliance outlet and customers walk the slightly undulating floors of the former offices and machine rooms.

The ground level where Chester and Grace worked remains, but is largely unused. Generations of wooden partitions break up the once-larger spaces whose windows are covered and where the lights are rarely turned on.

The park at Little York Lake continues to serve families that arrive with picnic lunches each summer. The tall pavilion which the traction company hoped would be its salvation now houses a summer theater serving all of Central New York.

Today the park is reached by automobile and is operated by the county. Dwyer Park is named for a former county officer whose

188

daughter-in-law made brief headlines in 1980 when she went to Iran during the hostage crisis and was, herself, arrested.

Most of the hotels that Chester and Grace used have succumbed to fire and urban expansion. The Tabor House in DeRuyter is gone along with the entire Lehigh Valley branch line that connected the town to Cortland. In Utica the Hotel Martin has been leveled. The old New York Central railroad station is dark and forbiding. Few trains stop and its halls echo with the footsteps of a handful of users.

The Alta Cliff Cottage stands in Tupper Lake, but its large, square mass is now broken into apartments. Its size and shape bear litttle resemblance to a "cottage." The hotel's original name must have been the creature of an advertising campaign to attract tourists sight unseen.

At Big Moose the Glennmore, like most Adirondack Hotels, burned leaving only its outbuildings. In one of these a successor carries on the Glennmore name as a restaurant. In Inlet the Arrowhead, too, has disappeared although its property serves as a public recreation area.

Big Moose Station, where Chester and Grace stepped from the train after the trip from Tupper Lake. The rail line is now abandoned; the station serves as a local restaurant.

189

The glistening Adirondack lakes still attract tourists in every season. Transients come by automobile and cottagers keep their docks and boats in the water from May to September. The principal state highway (Route 28) follows the Fulton Chain lakes, making them the new focus of tourism. Big Moose, once close to the summer action due to its rail station, is comfortably off in the backwater and its camp owners like it that way. Today the public is likely to read about Big Moose only in regard to acid rain problems, for it is one of the lakes hardest hit by this latest chapter of the industrial revolution.

Herkimer, the little city that was host to the great trial, remains a pleasant county seat and now hosts a community college. Violent crime is rare in this long county that thrusts deep into the Adirondacks, and locals still discuss the famous Gillette case as frequently as do their counterparts in Cortland.

The red courthouse remains, but the courtroom has been redecorated. The lighting is softer, the balcony is gone and so is the jury box cuspidor. The oppressive jail that housed Chester was itself condemned and now belongs to the Herkimer County Historical Society, which has renovated the building and opened it to the public.

Auburn prison remains as one of the walled, maximum security institutions administered by the New York State Department of Corrections. No longer do executions take place in Auburn. The chair in which Chester died disappeared. Rumors describe the chair being smuggled out of the prison during inmate riots of the 1920s.

INSTITUTIONS

The Russian fleet whose movements so captured the attention of American readers was annihilated by the Imperial Japanese Navy. Americans were most impressed but a generation later, in 1941, they had forgotten all about it.

The railroads changed drastically. The main line of the New York Central which was so busy in 1906 now schedules just four trains a day between Utica and New York City, all on *Amtrak*. To the North, the Adirondack Division fell apart, not once, but twice. In the 1960s the company abandoned the Montreal line as unprofitable, but in 1980 it briefly rose like Phoenix from the economic ashes of the depressed Northeast.

The roadbed was upgraded and track was laid. In a race against time the road was completed to serve the Winter Olympics at Lake

Placid. However, the season was brief and interest later waned. The rail line that took Chester and Grace to Big Moose fell once more into disuse. Today it belongs to legions of snowmobile enthusiasts.

Long before the Montreal route was abandoned the little station of Fulton Chain changed its name and spent its last years on the railroad as Thendara. By then the short spur to Old Forge was gone and today Thendara is just a jog in Route 28 where the old underpass stood. Most tourists barely notice the deserted depot and the rusting coaches standing on the siding.

The traction company lasted several more years in Cortland but ceased selling electric power to customers. It finally deserted its trolleys for busses, and in the nineteen fifties the nearly empty busses stopped running altogether.

The famous *Herald* supplement still lies in countless Cortland attics. It is yellowing and cracking at the seams but many families have kept it as the only souvenir of a story that happened in their grandparents' time. The *Herald* continues as the *Syracuse Herald Journal.* In Cortland, the *Cortland Standard* continues to publish every weekday, looking much like the *Standard* of 1906.

Alpha Delta sorority remained as the little normal school grew into a college. It eventually bought its own house and continued to be a campus force until a long decline set in among the Greek houses and in the late 1960s it ceased to exist.

Warner Brothers Company prospered in New York and Bridgeport, Connecticut. It saw the corset industry outgrow corsets and shrewdly anticipated the changes that came in the early twentieth century. Although it remained a family firm for many years it "went public" in 1961 under the name of Warnaco. It appears on the New York Stock Exchange as WRC and still makes high quality garments.[1]

The great New York to Paris automobile race ended in the summer of 1908 many weeks after Chester's execution. The American Thomas car, which had been heading for the Midwest as Chester died, arrived in Paris on July 31st and was declared the winner by twenty-six days. By now the race was front page news and the Gillette case was already slipping into the past.[2]

THE PEOPLE

Those who survived the drowning, the trial and the execution went about their own ways. Some were relatively unaffected by the events, others were never the same, but most drifted into obscurity. Several were destined to lead extremely unhappy lives of their own, and only a very few experienced success. Fewer yet rubbed shoulders with fame.

Erving E. Barnes, the Cortland police chief who accompanied officers from Herkimer County as they searched Chester's room remained something of a celebrity as he testified at the murder trial. Fifteen months later the police board brought charges against him. No specifications were made public but it was understood that he was to answer the charges at a regular meeting of the commission. Instead he submitted his resignation. The Commission accepted it, and Barnes disappeared from Cortland.[3]

Austin B. Klock, the undersheriff, was as close to Chester as any official in Herkimer County. He later became sheriff. He told and retold the story of the search for Chester and died in 1931 at the age of seventy-seven.[4]

Granville S. Ingraham, the deputy sheriff who was also involved in the search quickly cashed in on his big moment. A few months after the conviction, but while Chester was still in Auburn prison, Ingraham appeared as the author of a pamphlet published in Herkimer. It purported to be a history of the now famous murder case, but the greater portion of the publication was given over to Grace's letters. Chester's letters were conspicuously absent and few copies of the little book remain today.[5]

Bernice Ferrin left Auburn immediately after Chester's execution and returned to Zion City only to face a drama of her own. Her younger sister, Florence, had encountered a new religious experience—the Penticostal movement of Charles F. Parham. This particular trend of fundamental Christianity firmly believed that "speaking in tongues" was evidence of baptism by the Holy Spirit.

Little Zion City was filled with likely converts and young Florence was one of them. In a fit of despair following an argument with her father, she committed suicide by jumping into the nearby lake. Illinois newspapers treated the dramatic death as a tragedy brought on by unorthodox religion.

It was only six weeks since the execution and eastern newspapers which copied the story incorrectly assumed that Ferrin was the same young woman who had worked alongside Louise Gillette only two months earlier. It seemed like one more tragedy in the Gillette affair.

If so, it lay in the fact that Bernice had spent the spring months pleading for the life of Chester Gillette, while leaving Florence alone at home. Bernice helped her widowed father bury the younger sister and slipped quietly out of sight.[6]

George Washington Ward, who presented the state's case against Chester became county judge for the next term. By 1912 Ward eased himself into general practice and remained a solid member of the Herkimer County community until his death in Dolgeville.[7]

Albert Mills, the defense counsel quietly retreated from the notoriety of the trial. Senator Mills was already sixty-five years old but he lived in Herkimer County until his death in 1919.[8]

Myron Newman, the hotel keeper who took Chester into the Alta Cliff Cottage in Tupper Lake was in the Adirondacks for his health. He had left New York City with a severe asthma condition and sought out Saranac Lake for the "cure." Newman, who has been identified variously as Meyer, Myer and Myron, had migrated to Tupper Lake where he experimented with the hotel business and encountered Chester. By 1908 he had returned to New York City.

He might better have stayed in the mountains. He took a position as a jewelry salesman working on commission and then disappeared. Ransom letters demanding $10,000 for his release were received but Newman never reappeared.[9]

Carrie Gleason had visited Chester in the Herkimer jail and liked him. She was interested when her cousin Ed Curtis was chosen as a juror later in the year, but when the jury returned its verdict of "guilty" she was flabbergasted and for years to come she refused to set foot in the Curtis house in Illion.[10]

William J. Griffin had walked to town for up-to-date information on the Gillette trial. By 1907 the Griffin household was back to normal, although years later the older relatives would speak in hushed tones about the news that had come in the paper each November day, and how the poor young girl walked the porch of the Glenmore, crying and wringing her hands. Mr. Griffin lived for another half century and retired as a farmer but never again did he walk to the village merely to buy a newspaper.[11]

Bat Masterson continued to be a controversial New York sports writer. He continually blundered into scrapes and the *Morning Telegraph* was willing to put up with them. The old gunfighter had left Boot Hill far behind but when he died at his typewriter in 1921 he received a conventional New York ceremony.[12]

Dr. J. Mott Crumb and his wife Maude spent their lives in South Otselic. She died in 1944 and he in 1956. Both lie in a cemetery plot adjacent to Grace Brown's.

Royal K. Fuller, the newsman who saw the couple on the train and testified to that at the trial, drifted into public relations work, a natural outgrowth of journalism. In 1912 he introduced his assistant, Louis Howe, to young Franklin D. Roosevelt. The rising young New York State politician took Howe along with him on his way to becoming governor. Fuller served briefly as canal commissioner and generally worked in or around the state capital until 1935 when he committed suicide in his office.[13]

Charles Evans Hughes, the governor who turned down Louise Gillette's last personal appeals went on to fame and success. He became Secretary of State under Harding, was untouched by the Teapot Dome scandal and served as Chief Justice of the United States Supreme Court under several presidents.

Henry MacIlravy, Chester's spiritual advisor, remained a troubled young man. He returned to his congregation in Little Falls where many of his parishioners were skeptical of MacIlravy's relationship with the condemned man.

In November of 1908 MacIlravy spoke to his congregation in the little Southside Church. He saw for himself only two logical callings. One would be ministry in the prisons; the other a ministry to the leper colonies. The leper colonies seemed to be winning but Mr. MacIlravy slowly slipped from sight. It is doubtful that he followed either course of action.[14]

Dr. Edward Spitzka, the man who supervised the autopsy on Chester Gillette after the execution, built a national reputation as a brain specialist. But Spitzka suffered from alcoholism and, worse, he drifted into insanity. He resigned his position at the medical college and died of apoplexy at his Mt. Vernon, N. Y. home in 1922. He was only forty six years old.[15] The brain which he is reputed to have taken to Philadelphia has disappeared. Members of the faculty of the Jefferson University Medical School assume that if Chester's brain did arrive at their institution, it has long since been used by anatomy students after the college began to suffer a shortage of cadavers.[16]

Roy Higby, the boy who rode the steamboat on the search for Grace Brown grew up at Big Moose Lake and remained there as an adult. For years he ran the family property known as the Higby Club. Renowned throughout the Adirondacks as a storyteller, he finally committed his best tales to a small book called *A Man from the Past.*[17]

Hundreds of visitors and readers have pondered the fact that Higby's father carefully arranged that the boy would not be called as a trial witness. Years later lawyers who visited Higby mused over his

194

The small farmhouse in which Grace Brown grew up still stands on a hilltop in Chenango County.

account of grappling for the body with hooks. What the defense might have done with this information when explaining the damage to Billy Brown's head!

In the early years of television he appeared in a full page national advertisement for a manufacturer of television receivers, and looked out of the pages of the *National Geographic Magazine* with his mountain-bound television set in the background.[18]

George Washington Benham finished his term as warden of Auburn Prison and faded into anonymity. He was the second George Washington with whom Chester had to contend.

N. H. Gillette continued to operate the skirt factory for several years after the splash of notoriety afforded by Chester's trial. Harold and Leslie left for other regions and as the business began to decline much of the operation of the factory was given over to Dorothy Stanford, Gillette's married daughter. In 1916 Carrie Gillette died and N. H. was left alone. In 1920 when he was 65 years old, Horace married a woman in her thirties. They took a brief honeymoon in New England and shortly after returning home N. H. collapsed and died.[19]

Theresa Harnischfeger, who had watched Chester in the skirt factory and whose hour of glory came as a witness in the Herkimer trial enjoyed one more brief bit of notoriety. In the months after the trial she left her job at the Gillette Skirt Company and moved to Syracuse where she took another position. By summertime she was in the news again when it came to light that she had been secretly married. Such a serious breach of the 1907 code of ethics brought swift retaliation. Her employer quickly and properly discharged her and she slipped from public view![20]

Harold McGrath, the writer and copyreader from Syracuse continued to write for the rest of his life. He drifted into silent movies and put together scripts for *The Perils of Pauline*. He also left behind forty novels and an operetta when he died in 1932. His one bitter and vindictive bit of writing seems to have been contained in the paragraphs written after the trial conclusion when he wished that nothing would prevent Chester's execution.[21]

Theodore Dreiser did well with *An American Tragedy*. The novel sold, and while Dreiser flirted with an admiration for the new USSR during the twenties, he always managed to accept his royalties without pangs of guilt. He squabbled with his contemporaries, including H. L. Mencken and after watching World War II from the point of view of the Soviets, he quietly died in 1945. He is still the subject of countless monographs, although his literature is now considered to be heavy and tedious.

News notes about his famous novel still surface with regularity. *An American Tragedy* is still in print and the movies frequently replay on television. As recently as 1981, the *International Herald Tribune* of Paris drew from its files for its "Fifty Years Ago" column. It recalled Dreiser's unsuccessful suit to block the opening of the motion picture in 1931.[22]

Ruby Brown, Grace's youngest sister whose pet bird died in 1906 married in Central New York and lived longer than most of her contemporaries. By the 1980s she, along with Roy Higby, was one of the few principals left alive. She finally left New York State to live with a daughter in the South and died there in 1985, just one month short of her ninetieth birthday.

Harriet Benedict married a young lawyer in Cortland and raised her family in the community of her birth. Dreiser's novel brought a new generation of readers who assumed that she was the famous "Miss X." It was a trial she was to deal with for the rest of her life.

Chester's family returned to Colorado and quickly faded away. They never again appeared in national headlines.

Evelyn Nesbit recovered after taking poison in 1926. Like many entertainers before and since, suicide attempted was easier than suicide completed. The former actress died of old age in 1967, well over 81 years of age.

Harry K. Thaw changed his mind about the concept of the insanity plea and successfully evaded a murder conviction with one. He was committed to the Matteawan State Hospital for the criminally insane. In 1913 he escaped and made his way to Canada where he was captured and returned. He was later declared sane and was released for good in the 1920s. His wife divorced him and he lived out his life in relative quiet. He died of a heart attack at his home in Miami Beach in 1947. Chester had been dead for nearly forty years.[23]

Grace still lies in the family plot in the South Otselic Cemetery. The simple stone merely reads "At Rest."

Chester remains in his unmarked grave on the outskirts of Auburn. Today, few of the curious explore the cemetery seeking his grave and authorities are coyly secretive about its whereabouts. The quiet cemetery is probably the most peaceful place in which Chester ever slept.

Chester's resting place, in Soule Cemetery on the outskirts of Auburn, is located between the tree and the monument in the foreground in a row of unmarked graves. Grace lies in the family plot in South Otselic.

The Last Word—Then

Chester had a thousand judges and each seemed bent on rendering a judgment. For years after the trial and execution participants and total strangers freely dealt out their own accounts of the drowning and usually included a personal condemnation of Chester.

It was too late to ask Chester—he was gone forever. Still, he had taken the opportunity to make a final statement shortly before he died. When news came that his mother's personal appeal had been denied by Governor Hughes, reporters asked the inevitable and unnecessary question about how he felt. Chester replied:

> I don't believe that I am one hundredth part as bad as Harry Thaw, but there is nothing before me but the electric chair, and look at him with freedom just ahead of him. It isn't because he is any crazier than I am, but I am unfortunate enough to be born penniless. Hundreds saw him fire the bullet that killed White and they want to electrocute me on circumstantial evidence.[1]

Since Harry Thaw lived for many years and died in comparative luxury, Chester may be forgiven now for his bitterness toward the justice system. With the benefit of so many years of hindsight, one might even sympathize.

The Last Word—Now

Chester's affair with Grace Brown began in 1905, over eighty years ago. One would hope that some, at least, of the many questions might have been answered in the intervening years. Few have.

The question most frequently asked today is: "Do you think that Chester *really* did it?" One finds himself going through the same questions that must have plagued the twelve jurymen in 1906. Unfortunately the evidence is just as circumstantial today as it was then and the answer is just as unsatisfying—

No one really knows.

Notes

Chapter 1

1. *Cortland Standard,* July 5, 1906, p. 4.

Chapter 2

1. *The Combination Atlas Map of Cortland County,* p. 76.
2. Genealogy file, Cortland County Historical Society.
3. *General Catalog of Oberlin College 1908,* p. 372.
4. Jefferson County, Montana. Marriage records, handwritten entry, March 19, 1883.
5. *ibid.*

Chapter 3

1. Arthur W. Pearce, *The Future out of the Past,* (Privately published by the Warner Brothers Company, Bridgeport, Connecticut, 1964), p. 14.
2. Lucien Calvin Warner, *The Story of My Life,* (Privately published, New York City, 1914), pp. 93–94.
3. *ibid.,* p. 94.
4. *Cortland Standard,* September 18, 1920 (obituary).
5. *ibid.* August 26, 1916 (obituary).
6. *Directory of the City of Plainfield and North Plainfield for 1884–5,* (R. S. Dillon & Co.), p. 101.
7. *Brooklyn City Directory 1890–1891.*
8. *Brooklyn City Directory 1891–1892.*
9. Manuscript *Census of Cortland County, 1900.* Cortland City List, District 90, sheet B9.
10. "Grip," *Historical Souvenir of Cortland,* 1899, pp. 57–58.
11. *Cortland Standard,* January 8, 1904.
12. *ibid.* June 15, 1904.
13. "Grip," *op. cit.*
14. 1900 *Census, op. cit.*
15. *ibid.*

Chapter 4

1. Interview with Leonora DiPrima (Brown descendant), November 26, 1978.
2. Personal diary of Grace Brown, (1902), courtesy Dr. Robert C. Williams, Brooklyn, N. Y.
3. *ibid.*

4. *ibid.*
5. *ibid.*
6. M. C. Bond, *Changes in New York State Agriculture 1850–1950*, Dep. of Agricultural Economics, New York State College of Agriculture, Cornell University, A. E. 917, (Ithaca, N. Y., 1954), p. 4.
7. Letter from Leslie E. Bell, Chenango County Real Property Tax Services, February 11, 1981.
8. Manuscript Census of Cortland County 1905, First Ward, p. 31.

Chapter 5

1. *Cortland Standard*, March 23, 1908.
2. Abstract of Salvation Army Records accompanying a letter from Judith Johnson, Assistant Archivist, Archives and Research Center, The Salvation Army, June 11, 1982.
3. *ibid.*
4. W. P. A., Federal Writers' Program, *The New Washington*, (Portland, Oregon, 1941), pp. 178–181.
5. Abstract, *op. cit.*
6. *ibid.*
7. Howard M. Brier, *Sawdust Empire*, (Knopf, New York, 1958), pp. 79–85.
8. Abstract, *op. cit.*
9. W. P. A., *op. cit.*, pp. 364–365.
10. *The War Cry*, various issues, 1898.
11. Abstract, *op. cit.*
12. *ibid.*
13. W. P. A., Federal Writers' Program, *Wyoming*, (Oxford University Press, New York, 1941), pp. 142–143.
14. W. P. A., Federal Writers' Project, *California*, (Hastings House, New York, 1939), pp. 466–467.
15. *The War Cry*, September 15, 1900, p. 12.
16. *ibid.*, October 6, 1900, p. 12.
17. *Catalog of Oberlin College 1901–1902*, (Oberlin, Ohio), p. 215.
18. Oberlin Academic Record for Chester Gillette, p. 164.
19. *Cortland Standard*, November 20, 1906, (N. H. Gillette testimony).
20. Elmer T. Clark, *The Small Sects in America*, (Abingdon Press, New York, 1937), pp. 154–156.
21. Oberlin Academic Record, *op. cit.*
22. Original in the archives of Oberlin College Library.
23. *Cortland Standard*, November 20, 1906, *op. cit.*
24. *ibid.*, April 3, 1905.
25. *The People of New York State v. Chester Gillette*, (Trial manuscript, 1906), p. 1006. (Hereafter refered to as Trial ms.)

204

Chapter 6

1. *Cortland Standard,* November 20, 1908, *op. cit.*
2. *ibid.,* April 3, 1905.
3. George Hanford, *Cortland, Homer and McGrawville Directory, 1906* (Elmira, N. Y., 1906), p. 100.
4. *Cortland Standard,* June 15, 1904.
5. *ibid.,* November 20, 1906, (Harold Gillette testimony)
6. *ibid.,* June 15, 1904.
7. *Cortland Democrat,* November 23, 1906, (Theresa Harnispheger testimony).
8. *ibid.,* (Ada Hawley Testimony).
9. Trial ms., pp. 1007–1009.
10. *ibid.*
11. *ibid.,* p. 1007.
12. *Cortland Standard,* November 19, 1906, (Carrie Wheeler testimony).
13. *Cortland Democrat, op. cit.*
14. Trial ms., pp. 1011–1014.
15. *ibid.*
16. *ibid.,* pp. 1009–1010.
17. *ibid.,* pp. 1015–1017.
18. *The People of New York State v. Chester Gillette,* (Appeal Record, 1908) pp. 704–705, (Trial Exhibit 98, Post Mortem notes). (Hereafter refered to as Appeal Record.)

Chapter 7

1. *Cortland Standard,* November 20, 1906, (George Hoag testimony).
2. *ibid.,* (Alfred B. Raymond testimony).
3. *ibid.,* (Robert Wilcox testimony).
4. *Cortland Democrat,* November 23, 1906 (Carrie Wheeler testimony).
5. *D. L. & W. Timetable* (Cincinnatus Branch), effective December 1, 1905.
6. Trial ms., pp. 1018–1020.
7. *ibid.*
8. *ibid.*
9. *ibid.*
10. *ibid.,* pp. 1022–1024.
11. *ibid.*
12. *ibid.*
13. *ibid.,* p. 1025.
14. *ibid.,* pp. 1026–1028.
15. *ibid.,* pp. 1029–1033.
16. *ibid.*
17. *ibid.*
18. *Cortland Standard,* July 16, 1906 (news story).
19. *ibid.,* November 20, 1906 (Minnie Hogan testimony).

20. Trial ms., pp. 1037–1038.
21. *ibid.*
22. *ibid.*, pp. 1038–1042.
23. *ibid.*, pp. 1043–1046.
24. *ibid.*, pp. 1050–1051.
25. *ibid.*, pp. 1046–1049.
26. *ibid.*, pp. 1050–1051.
27. *ibid.*, pp. 1054–1057.

Chapter 8

1. *Cortland Standard*, November 20, 1906 (Ella Hoag testimony).
2. *ibid.*, (N. H. Gillette testimony).
3. *ibid.*
4. *ibid.*, (Maude Crumb testimony).
5. *Cortland Standard*, November 21, 1906 (Ralph F. Weaver testimony).
6. Edith Cornwall, *Syracuse Herald Supplement*, (Syracuse, December 9, 1906), p. 4.
7. Appeal Record, p. 691 (Trial Exhibit 32).
8. *Cortland Standard*, November 21, 1906 (Mrs. Myra Coye testimony).
9. *ibid.*, (Harold Williams testimony).
10. *ibid.*, (Josephine Patrick testimony).
11. *ibid.*, (John A. Pallas testimony).
12. Appeal Record, pp. 692–694 (Trial Exhibit 34).
13. *Cortland Standard*, November 21, 1906 (WIlliam M. Martin testimony).
14. Appeal Record, pp. 692–694.
15. *Cortland Standard*, November 21, 1906 (Guy Zimmerman testimony).
16. Mark Sullivan, *Our Times*, (Charles Scribner's, New York, 1930) pp. 444–451.
17. *Cortland Standard*, November 21, 1906 (Myron Newman testimony).
18. Appeal Record, pp. 694–695 (Trail Exhibit 39).
19. *Cortland Standard*, November 21, 1906 (Clara Greenwood testimony).
20. Newman testimony, *op. cit.*
21. Greenwood testimony, *op. cit.*
22. Interview with Mr. J. Edward "Ed" Timmons of Tupper Lake, September 4, 1977.
23. Appeal Record, pp. 688–689 (Trial Exhibit 23).
24. *ibid.*, p. 687 (Trial Exhibit 4).
25. *Cortland Standard*, November 21, 1906 (James McAllister testimony).
26. Appeal Record, p. 687 (Trial Exhibit 4 and 23).
27. *Cortland Standard*, November 22, 1906 (Andrew Morrison testimony).
28. Appeal Record, pp. 696–697 (Trial Exhibit 52).
29. *Cortland Standard*, November 22, 1906 (Robert Morrison testimony).
30. Letter from Jean Brown Etheridge to Professor Raymond Malbone of SUNY Cortland, July 23, 1966.
31. Roy C. Higby, *A Man from the Past*, (Big Moose Press, Big Moose, N. Y., 1974) p. 140.

Chapter 9

1. *Cortland Standard*, November 29, 1906 (Chester Gillette testimony).
2. *ibid.*, November 22, 1906 (James S. Hart testimony).
3. *ibid.*, (Albert J. Stiles testimony).
4. Appeal Record, pp. 697–698 (Trial Exhibit 57).
5. *ibid.*, pp. 687–688 (Trial Exhibit 5).
6. *ibid.*, p. 699 (Trial Exhibit 67).
7. *Cortland Standard*, November 22, 1906 (Frank Williams testimony).
8. *ibid.*, (Gertrude Dean testimony).
9. *ibid.*, (Albert C. Boshart testimony).
10. Gertrude Dean testimony, *op. cit.*
11. *Cortland Standard*, November 21, 1906 (Leon J. Hoffman testimony).
12. Appeal Record, p. 694 (Trial Exhibit 38).
13. *Cortland Standard*, July 13, 1906, p. 6.
14. Granville S. Ingraham, *The Gillette Murder Trial*, (Charles E. Garlock, Herkimer, N. Y., 1907), p. 10.
15. *The Journal*, (Newport, N. Y.) July 20, 1906, p. 1.
16. Granville S. Ingraham, *op. cit.*
17. *ibid.*, pp. 10–11.
18. *ibid.*
19. *ibid.*
20. *ibid.*, p. 12.
21. *ibid.*, p. 13.
22. *ibid.*
23. *ibid.*
24. *ibid.*
25. *ibid.*
26. *The Journal*, *op. cit.*

Chapter 10

1. *Cortland Standard*, July 17, 1906, p. 1.
2. *The New York Times*, July 15, 1906, p. 5.
3. *ibid.*, July 16, 1906, p. 4.
4. *Cortland Standard*, November 20, 1906 (Erving E. Barnes testimony).
5. *ibid.*, (Lizzie Crain testimony).
6. *Cortland Standard*, July 17, 1906, p. 5.
7. *ibid.*, p. 1.
8. *ibid.*, July 21, 1906, p. 6.
9. *ibid.*, July 23, 1906, p. 6.
10. *ibid.*, July 21, 1906. p. 6.
11. *ibid.*
12. *ibid.*, July 26, 1906, p. 6.
13. *ibid.*, July 28, 1906, p. 6.
14. *ibid.*, July 31, 1906, p. 6.
15. *ibid.*

16. Interview with Iva Neugebauer (Carrie's niece), July 11, 1983.
17. *Cortland Democrat,* August 10, 1906, p. 1.
18. *Cortland Standard,* August 13, 1906, p. 5.
19. *ibid.,* August 25, 1906, p. 6.
20. *ibid.,* August 11, 1906, p. 5.
21. *Herkimer Telegram,* August 13, 1906.
22. *Cortland Standard,* August 10, 1906.
23. *ibid.,* August 18, 1906, p. 6.
24. *ibid.,* August 23, 1906, p. 5.
25. *ibid.,* August 29, 1906, p. 5.
26. *ibid.,* August 31, 1906, p. 6.
27. *ibid.*
28. *ibid.,* October 19, 1906, p. 6.

Chapter 11

1. *Cortland Standard,* November 14, 1906, p. 1.
2. *ibid.,* November 13, 1906, p. 1.
3. Granville S. Ingraham, *op. cit.,* p. 71.
4. *Cortland Standard, op. cit.*
5. *ibid.*
6. *ibid.,* November 14, 1906, p. 1.
7. Neugebauer interview, *cit.*
8. *Cortland Standard,* November 13, 1906, p. 1.
9. *ibid.,* November 16, 1906, p. 1.
10. *ibid.*
11. Appeal Record, pp. 473–476.
12. *Cortland Standard,* November 17, 1906, p. 1.
13. Appeal Record, *op. cit.*
14. Trial ms., p. 791–812.
15. Trial ms., p. 1052 (Trial Exhibit 21) and p. 1045 (Trial Exhibit 19).
16. *Cortland Standard,* November 17, 1906, p. 2.
17. *Cortland Standard,* November 20, 1906, p. 1.
18. Richard G. Case, "She was Colorful," in the Syracuse *Herald American.*
19. *Cortland Standard,* November 20, 1906, p. 1.

Chapter 12

1. Appeal Record, pp. 62–63.
2. *Cortland Standard,* November 19, 1906, p. 2.
3. Appeal Record, pp. 689–690 (Trial Exhibit 30).
4. Trial ms., pp. 1058–1066.
5. Interview with Frederick Griffin (son of W. J. Griffin), July 3, 1983.
6. Appeal Record, pp. 65–66 (Witness List).
7. *ibid.,* p. 66.

8. *ibid.*
9. *ibid.*
10. *ibid.*
11. *ibid.,* pp. 66–67.
12. *ibid.,* p. 67.
13. Appeal Record, pp. 695–697 (Trial Exhibit 52).
14. *ibid.,* pp. 68–69 (Witness List).
15. *ibid.,* p. 68.
16. *ibid.,* p. 69.
17. *Cortland Standard,* November 21, 1906, p. 1.
18. *ibid.,* November 22, 1906, p. 1.
19. Appeal Record, p. 681 (Exhibit List).
20. *ibid.,* p. 686.
21. *ibid.*
22. *ibid.*
23. *ibid.,* (Trial Exhibit 99).
24. Roy C. Higby, *op. cit.,* p. 142.
25. Appeal Record, p. 71 (Witness List).
26. *ibid.,* p. 706.
27. *Cortland Standard,* November 27, 1906, p. 1.

Chapter 13

1. *Cortland Standard,* November 24, 1906, p. 1.
2. *ibid.*
3. *ibid.,* November 28, 1906, p. 1.
4. *ibid.,* November 30, 1906, p. 1.
5. *ibid.*
6. *ibid.*
7. *ibid.,* December 1, 1906, p. 1.
8. *ibid.*
9. *ibid.*
10. Ingraham, *op. cit.,* pp. 42–56.
11. *ibid.*
12. *ibid.,* pp. 57–66.
13. *Cortland Standard,* December 4, 1906, p. 1.
14. Ingraham, *op. cit.,* p. 68.
15. *ibid.,* p. 70.
16. *ibid.*
17. *Cortland Democrat,* December 14, 1906, p. 1.

Chapter 14

1. *Syracuse Herald Supplement,* p. 2.
2. *ibid.,* back cover.
3. *Cortland Standard,* December 8, 1906.
4. *ibid.,* December 10, 1906.

5. *ibid.,* December 11, 1906.
6. *Herkimer Telegram,* December 13, 1906.
7. Dale T. Schoenberger, *The Gunfighters,* (Caxton Printers, Caldwell, Idaho, 1971) pp. 130–131.
8. *Cortland Standard,* December 13, 1906.
9. *ibid.,* December 15, 1906.
10. *ibid.,* January 11, 1907.
11. *ibid.,* February 8, 1907.
12. Letter from Mrs. Francis P. Walsh (childhood memories), January 22, 1977. For variations and other verses see Harold W. Thompson, *Body, Boots and Britches,* J. B. Lippincott, Philadelphia, 1939) pp. 443–445.
13. Maude E. Gould, "Entreating," published by Maude E. Gould, Illion, N. Y., 1907.
14. *Cortland Standard,* February 7, 1907.
15. Original in the Herkimer County Historical Society.
16. *Cortland Standard,* January 10, 1908.
17. *Syracuse Herald,* Febuary 19, 1908, p. 1.
18. *People of New York State v. Chester Gillette (Appellant),* (New York Reports, 1908) pp. 107–109.
19. *Syracuse Herald,* February 20, 1908, p. 1.
20. *ibid.,* Feburary 19, 1908.
21. *ibid.,* March 1, 1908.
22. *Herkimer Telegram,* March 7, 1908.
23. *Cortland Standard,* March 30, 1908.
24. *Century Magazine,* May 1902 to October 1902.
25. *Cortland Standard,* March 17, 1908.
26. *ibid.,* March 28, 1908.
27. *ibid.,* March 29, 1908.
28. *The Post Standard* (Syracuse), March 30, 1908.

Chapter 15

1. *The Post Standard, op. cit.,* p. 2.
2. *Cortland Standard,* March 30, 1908, p. 1.
3. *The Post Standard,* March 27, 1908, p. 1.
4. *Auburn Daily Advertiser,* March 30, 1908, pp. 1–7.
5. *The Post Standard,* March 30, 1908, p. 1.
6. *ibid.*
7. *ibid.*
8. *Auburn Daily Advertiser, op. cit.*
9. *Saturday Globe* (Utica), April 4, 1908, p. 1.
10. *Auburn Daily Advertiser, op. cit.*
11. Typewritten copy of post mortem report in Auburn Prison files.
12. *The New York Times* (obituary), Dr. Edward Spitzka, September 6, 1922.
13. Post Mortem Report, *op. cit.*

14. Typewritten copy of statement to Warden Benham from Henry MacIlravy and Cordello Herrick.
15. Typewritten copy in Auburn Prison files.
16. Tallman Undertaking Establishment, funeral record #5774, March 31, 1908.
17. Typewritten copy of order from Chester Gillette to Warden G. W. Benham, (undated).
18. *Cortland Standard*, April 6, 1908.
19. *ibid.*, December 30, 1908.
20. *Syracuse Herald*, November 25, 1923, Section 3, p. 5.

Chapter 16

1. W. A. Swanberg, *Dreiser*, (Charles Scribner's Sons, New York, 1965), p. 4.
2. *ibid.*, pp. 4–5.
3. *ibid.*, pp. 5–16.
4. F. O. Matthiessen, *Theodore Dreiser* (William Sloane Associates, 1951), p. 15.
5. Swanberg, *op. cit.*, pp. 7, 12–13, 51.
6. *ibid.*, p. 74.
7. Kenneth W. Leish (editor), *The American Heritage Songbook*, (The American Heritage Publishing Company, New York), p. 197.
8. Swanberg, *op. cit.*, pp. 80–93.
9. Peter Schwed, *God Bless Pawnbrokers*, (Dodd, Mead and Company, New York, 1975), p. 48.
10. Swanberg, *op. cit.*, p. 118.
11. *ibid.*, pp. 253–254.
12. Philip L. Gerber, *Theodore Dreiser*, (Twayne Publishers, Boston, 1964), p. 129.
13. Helen Dreiser, *My Life with Dreiser*, (World, New York, 1951), pp. 71–85.
14. *ibid.*
15. Swanberg, *op. cit.*, pp. 286–287.
16. *ibid.*, pp. 295–296.
17. Jack Salzman (editor), *Theodore Dreiser, The Critical Reception*, (David Lewis, New York, 1972), pp. 451–454.
18. *New York Herald Tribune*, January 3, 1926.
19. *Cortland Standard*, January 5, 1926, p. 5.
20. *ibid.*, p. 1.
21. *ibid.*, January 7, 1926, p. 8.

Chapter 17

1. Theodore Dreiser, *An America Tragedy*, (World Publishing Company, New York, 1953). This paperback edition is most likely to be found by the modern reader.

211

2. Ingraham, *op. cit.*, p. 67.
3. Dreiser, *op. cit.*, p. 736.
4. *ibid.*, pp. 663–664.

Chapter 18

1. Ruth Epperson Kennel, *Theodore Dreiser and the Soviet Union 1927–1945,* (International Publishers, New York, 1969), p. 43.
2. Helen Dreiser, *op. cit.*, pp. 121–123.
3. *The New York Times*, August 6, 1931, p. 22 (Review).
4. *ibid.*, July 16, 1931, p. 19.
5. *ibid.*, March 24, 1934, p. 9.
6. *ibid.*, August 29, 1951, p. 20 (Review).
7. *Cleveland Plain Dealer Magazine*, November 1, 1931, p. 2.
8. *The Post Standard*, May 14, 1950.
9. *The American Weekly*, undated, pp. 30–31.
10. *Syracuse Herald Journal*, July 3, 1963.
11. *Evening Telegram*, (St. John's, Newfoundland), September 16, 1966.
12. *Syracuse Herald American, Empire Magazine*, April 30, 1967, pp. 10–12.
13. Higby, *op. cit.*, pp. 137–143.

Chapter 19

1. Pearce, *op. cit.*, pp. 52–53.
2. *The New York Times*, July 31, 1908, p. 7.
3. *Cortland Standard*, September 19, 1907.
4. *The New York Times*, October 19, 1931, p. 21.
5. Ingraham, *op. cit.*
6. *Waukegan Daily Sun*, May 25, 1908, p. 1.
7. Biographical notes from the Herkimer County historical Society. By letter, June 28, 1984.
8. *ibid.*
9. *The New York Times*, June 29, 1908, p. 10.
10. Neugebauer, Inteview *cit.*
11. Interview with Frederick Griffin, Oswegatchie, New York, July 3, 1983.
12. Dumas Malone (editor, *Dictionary of America Biography, Vol. 12* (Charles Scribner's Sons, New York, 1933) pp. 383–384.
13. *The New York Times*, September 14, 1935, p. 3 (obituary).
14. Clipping file, Herkimer County Historical Society. By letter, June 28, 1984.
15. Edward L. Bauer, *Doctors Made in America*, (Lippincott, Philadelphia, 1963), pp. 278–280.
16. Letter from Andrew Ramsay, Emeritus Professor of Anatomy, Jefferson Medical College, September 9, 1982.
17. Higby, *op. cit.*

18. *National Geographic Magazine,* May 1952.
19. *Cortland Standard,* September 18, 1920.
20. *ibid.,* May 20, 1907.
21. *The Post Standard,* October 30, 1932.
22. *International Herald Tribune* (Paris), August 7, 1981.
23. *The New York Times,* February 23, 1947, p. 53 (obituary).

The Last Word

1. *Cortland Standard,* February 27, 1908, p. 5.

Illustration Credits

Composed on a Franklin Ace 1000 computer
   using the Acewriter word processing program.

Typeset in 10½ point Palatino with a baseline of 12
   on a Itek Digitek 3000 photocompositor.

Printed on 60 pound book white
   and bound in a 10 point coated-one-side cover
   by McNaughton & Gunn, Inc.

Cover graphics by Christopher Wolff.

Contact Walt Steesy for your book publishing needs.

A *quality* publication from
Heart of the Lakes Publishing
Interlaken, New York 14847

The Family of
Chester Gillette

| John Gillett (1757–1838) Mary Benedict (1754–1846) | Horatio Gillett (1799–1885) Marilla Starr (1797–1870) |

| Noah Humphrey Osborne (1802–1894) Eliza A. Thompson (1805–1881) |

Not all children have been shown, nor has any attempt been made to continue the family beyond the generation of Chester Gillette.